A SYSTEMS APPROACH
TO HANDICAPPED CHILDREN

A SYSTEMS
APPROACH TO
HANDICAPPED
CHILDREN

HELPING CHILDREN GROW

LAUREN CARLILE BRADWAY PH.D.

CHARLES C THOMAS · PUBLISHER · SPRINGFIELD · ILLINOIS

RJ
496
.L4
B73
1984

Published and Distributed Throughout the World by

CHARLES C THOMAS • PUBLISHER
2600 South First Street
Springfield, Illinois 62717

© *1984 by* CHARLES C THOMAS • PUBLISHER

ISBN 0-398-05025-2
Library of Congress Catalog Card Number: **84-8656**

With THOMAS BOOKS *careful attention is given to all details of manufacturing and
design. It is the Publisher's desire to present books that are satisfactory as to their physical
qualities and artistic possibilities and appropriate for their particular use.* THOMAS
BOOKS *will be true to those laws of quality that assure a good name and good will.*

Printed in the United States of America
SC-R-3

Library of Congress Cataloging in Publication Data

Bradway, Lauren Carlile.
  A systems approach to handicapped children.

  Bibliography: p.
  Includes index.
  1. Handicapped children—Care and treatment.
2. Handicapped children—Education.   3. System theory.
4. Children—Diseases—Diagnosis.   5. Child psychopathology—Diagnosis.   6. Socially handicapped children.
I. Title.
RJ138.B73   1984   618.92   84-8656
ISBN 0-398-05025-2

For *Howard, Jan,* and *Larry*—the ones who never doubted I could write this book.

FOREWORD

It has been a great pleasure to me to find that work done at an earlier time—ideas developed, meetings organized around the topic of general systems theory and psychiatry, and the "state of the art" book that followed from this, *General Systems Theory and Psychiatry* (first published by Little, Brown, Boston in 1969 and republished by Intersystems Publications, Seaside, California in 1981)—has served as a stimulus to a number of people. I believe that the book was important, and evidently my colleagues also saw something of importance in it, as the first edition sold out. Mark Davidson, author of *Uncommon Sense,* a biography of the founder of general systems theory, Ludwig von Bertalanffy (Los Angeles: Tarcher 1983), felt that the book was valuable in his apprehending the humanistic aspects of von Bertalanffy's work.

My continuing work on the humanistic aspects of general systems theory and my development of a general systems theory of the emotional origin of thought, which I called emotional-cognitive structure theory, contributed to the work of Paul LaViolette in evolving emotional-perceptive cycling theory and to his immersion in the task of editing posthumously the unpublished work of von Bertalanffy in *A Systems View of Man* (Boulder, Colorado: Westview Press, 1981).

I have known that the system precursor/system forming view of systems has led to important results in ethology, philosophy, understanding of man-environment relations and to joint continuing work with Aristide H. Esser, founder of The Association for the Study of Man-Environment Relations and developer of an Ecology of Knowledge Network. These system precursor/system forming concepts have been incorporated by the philosopher Jerzy A. Wojciechowski in his view of human knowledge as a system forming system to which man has only an ecological relationship.

vii

From this foundation Wojciechowski has forwarded the very important formulation of the ecology of knowledge. Esser in his work has incorporated the notion of brain-behavior-environment relationships, tieing in Paul MacLean's work on the basic concept of the triune brain, done in the Laboratory of Brain Evolution and Behavior at the National Institute of Mental Health. The system precursor/system forming view fits well also with the work of the ethologist Michael Chance. But within the last year it has been especialy nice to have surprises show up in the form of books by other authors citing my work as an important foundation to their own thinking. Two of these are Lauren Carlile Bradway and Bunny S. Duhl.

Lauren Carlile Bradway, in her book, *A Systems Approach to Handicapped Children: Helping Children Grow,* does not mention these more recent developments, but the theme and tenor of her book are in line with them. I would consider that even though she may be unaware of the developments in this field she does contribute to the area of the ecology of knowledge, as illustrated by her admirable chapter on "The Ecology of Evaluation."

In the field of family therapy Bunny Duhl's book, *From the Inside Out and Other Metaphors: Creative and Integrative Approaches to Training in Systems Thinking*, was published by Brunner/Mazel in 1983. I was most delighted with the author's statement, tracing her introduction to general systems theory through her husband, that "Fred Duhl's meeting with psychiatrist Bill Gray in the early 1960s provided him with his first awareness of general systems theory, which seemed to make room for an integration of his range of concerns and interests. He became an active explorer of general systems theory."

Dr. Bradway ascribes what I have written and published as an important origin of the further development of general systems theory in her work. It is particularly pleasing to me that she recognizes the aim of general systems theory as that of integrating the systems sciences and the disciplinary sciences to provide a new type of approach in which humanistic values are required and take high priority. As I have noted this was essential to von Bertalanffy and also to me in the work I did to extend this humanistic trend. I am equally pleased that Dr. Bradway has adopted the view I have forwarded for many years of regarding the human being as a system ecologically suspended in multiple systems. She states, "The child is ecologically suspended in multiple systems. So embedded is the child in this environmental matrix that it becomes impossible to separate one from the other." Elsewhere she emphasizes, "When we see a handicapped child, the learning problem to be defined is not bounded by the child. We look at all systems, enlarging the boundary of the problem to include family, school and community." With great clarity and force she develops this concept of the child as a system, an approach which has not been duplicated in the general systems literature.

As a matter of parallel evolution, it is interesting to me that on the day I am writing this Foreword I have heard a talk by Lois Slovik, M.D., a pediatrician turned psychiatrist, director of family therapy for children at the Massachusetts General Hospital in Boston. She speaks of the symptom bearing child as suspended in a number of matrices of which the family is the most important. Thus the parallel to Bradway's ecological matrices in which the primary system will be school, for Lauren Carlile Bradway in this book has prepared the leading edge for the application of general systems theory to education as the Duhls and others have done for family therapy.

Dr. Bradway brings a new perspective and understanding to an area that has remained puzzling and often hopeless for many people. It is no surprise that she states in her Preface that her "greatest desire as a student and as a teacher has always been to *understand.*" She explains that "By simplifying, clarifying and unifying information, General Systems Theory has the amazing ability to aid understanding." I agree most heartily, for this is what attracted me to the field in the late 1950s. Bradway's aim in writing this book is to share the helpfulness of the systems perspective with the students who are training to work with children as diagnosticians, teachers and therapists, general systems theory being presented as a perspective for evaluation and treatment of children with learning problems. Since it emphasizes wholes and synthesis rather than parts and analysis she uses it in an admirable way to offer an alternative to the present labeling of children, or the searching for a single cause of the child's handicap.

Most effectively Dr. Bradway carries out the task suggested by Kenneth Boulding in 1956, when he referred to general systems theory as "the skeleton of a science"; she fleshes out the skeleton with information from child growth and development, embryology, genetics, psychology, anthropology, social psychology, psycholinguistics and human ecology. She utilizes both Anatol Rapoport's "soft definition" of a system as a "portion of the world that is perceived as a unit and that is able to maintain its 'identity' in spite of changes going on within it," and Talcott Parsons' conceptualization of the "role" rather than the individual as the smallest unit of a social system. With equal effectiveness she puts into practice the synthetic orientation of general systems theory, interweaving her formal explanations with very well chosen clinical material. This makes her book both very enjoyable to read and very helpful to the students and practitioners of the various professions involved in helping the handicapped child grow.

Using James G. Miller's levels of living systems and focusing on the in common characteristics of all systems with which the child is involved—biological, psychological and social—she chooses for special study the elements of input, throughput, output, vital balance and system distress. The latter two are usually not dealt with in a specific enough fashion. Vital balance, a concept highlighted by Gordon Allport, Karl Menninger and Augustin de la Peña, (author of *The Psychobiology of Cancer,* Praeger, 1983), deals with the tension producing and tension reducing qualities of human beings, encompassing Ludwig von Bertalanffy's insistence on the primary status of spontaneous activity in the growth and development of living systems and in creativity, reactivity being secondary.

System distress has been highlighted in the work of Stephen Fleck, and although distress in one system will spread to others, it is still important to evaluate the particular system being primarily distressed. In my own terminology I would characterize the maintenance of vital balance or the appearance of system distress as related to rich relevant nurturing environments, including the resources of time, money and professionalism on the one hand, and insufficient relevant nurturing environments on the other. System distress that is devastating includes mental retardation, autism and terminal illness. Disruption of the status quo, however, may be important to maintaining a vital balance, in line with von Bertalanffy's insistence that spontaneous activity, not homeostasis, is a good model for growth.

In her chapter on "Ways Children Learn" Dr. Bradway highlights the importance of auditory, visual and tactile stimuli, pointing out that from birth the infant will seek out stimulation and even work for it, the seeking of stimulation achieving the status of a drive or motivational tendency not unlike that of hunger. This coincides with de la Peña's hypothesis of boringness as pathology producing and his notion that new information is necessary food for the brain. Bradway provides excellent detail on the importance of attending, pointing out that the way to get and hold the attention of a child is by manipulating the quantity and quality of information in the environment. All levels of living systems prefer inputs which are intense, spatially extensive, moving, changing, repeated a few times and colorful—or in other words, complex and high in informational content. She thus ties in her practical observations with the theoretical contributions of James G. Miller, Augustin de la Peña and Eric Jantsch, who pointed out the need to avoid the extremes of stimulation underload or total confirmation, which would lead to death, and total novelty, which would mean chaos. In this chapter Bradway goes on to define input-output types in terms of listening-speaking, looking-acting and touching-interacting. She points out that hearing impaired children substitute listening/looking-speaking for listening-speaking.

Lauren Carlile Bradway's new book is a critical advance in our approach to the conceptualization of handicapped children and it greatly enhances our ability to help them grow. I would predict that it will become a classic in the literature, an essential textbook for all of those involved in dealing with handicapped children, including teachers and students in the wide variety of professions involved, families and self help groups, health and treatment planners and the general public. Reflecting on the derivation of the word "handicap," a lottery game in which winners were penalized by having their hand in a cap, one could say that Bradway takes the hand out of the cap for handicapped children by making educational treatment a high priority for them. In my three readings of this fascinating book I find myself admiring the comprehensiveness in the range of areas she deals with. Her skill in understanding and being able to use the synthetic and synergic elements of general systems theory increase both the value of her book and the pleasure one has in reading it. And finally, the excellent illustrations by Susan Small enhance and clarify the text.

William Gray, M.D.
Private Practice of Psychiatry
Newton Center, Massachusetts

PREFACE

My intent in writing this book has been to provide those of you who are in training to teach handicapped children with a perspective for your work. The book is not intended to be comprehensive in any way. Every one of the hundreds of topics touched upon in the following pages (such as genetics, embryology, language development) could fill books in themselves. The handicaps mentioned (like autism, cerebral palsy, learning disabilities) would require volumes to cover adequately.

My greatest desire as a student and as a teacher has always been to *understand.* By simplifying, clarifying, and unifying information, General Systems Theory has the amazing ability to aid understanding. Because the systems perspective has been so helpful to me, I'm happy to be able to share it now with you.

In writing this book, I am indebted to the hundreds of children I've worked with over the past 12 years in my role of speech-language pathologist. While teaching them to communicate more clearly and to read, spell, and do math, I've learned so much from them.

I became excited about the field of speech-language pathology while I was a graduate student at Central Missouri State University in Warrensburg, Missouri, thanks to the enthusiasm of Lin Welch, Ph.D., chairman of the department. I am grateful to my professors in the Department of Human Ecology at the University of Oklahoma Health Sciences Center for introducing me to General Systems Theory. They are: Jim Allen, M.D., Tulsa, Oklahoma; Jay Shurley, M.D., Oklahoma City; and the late Bob Hood, Ph.D.

Thanks to those who helped in the actual production of the book: Susan Small, for the lively illustrations; Sherry Gillespie, for the expert editing and typing; and Theo Kerns, for her many hours of careful proofreading with me. During the two years I worked on the manuscript, my friend, Jan Tucker, and my husband, Howard, were there at the times when I hit a snag in my writing. Understanding that once is not always enough, they patiently listened to some of my problems through the third and fourth telling.

A number of people generously shared their expertise with me. They are Tom Finn, M.D., pediatrician and allergist; Duncan Threlkeld, M.D., obstetrician and gynecologist; Elizabeth Hodgen, lay midwife; Becky McBride, neonatal nurse; and Johnnie Mae Lovato, Navajo Indian. Effie Poe, my grandmother, and Bridget Bradway, my sister-in-law, took time to relate personal anecdotes about bringing up children.

And finally, my thanks to two significant people: Payne Thomas, of Charles C Thomas, Publisher, who has given me the opportunity to share my experiences with you, and William Gray, M.D., one of my long-time systems heroes, who so graciously consented to write a foreword to this book.

Lauren Carlile Bradway, Ph.D.
Private Practice
Oklahoma City, Oklahoma

CONTENTS

PART II: THE BIOLOGICAL SYSTEM

PART V: CONCLUSION

Chapter

A SYSTEMS APPROACH
TO HANDICAPPED CHILDREN

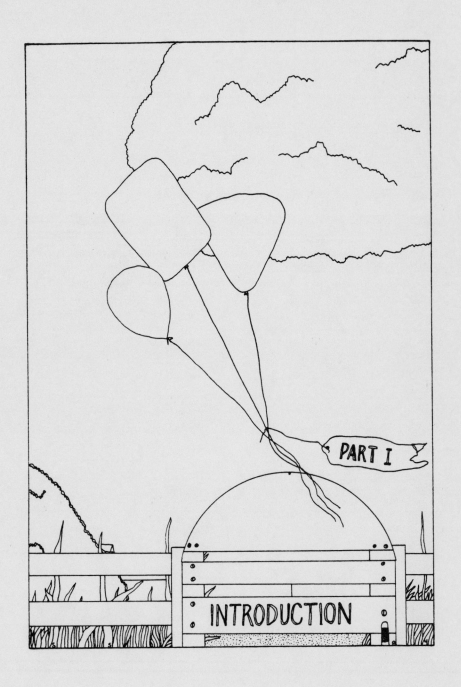

Chapter 1

THE CHILD AS A SYSTEM

Michael Patterson at three-and-a-half is a freckled-faced little boy with red hair. His entire expressive vocabulary consists of "mama," "home," "mine," and "boat," and he'll say none of these words when asked. Sue Patterson, his mother, has made an appointment for Michael with a psychologist for a diagnostic evaluation. At the intake interview, she explains to Dr. Warren that her family doctor assured her that Michael would outgrow his problems, but she's no longer sure that he's right.

In his interview with Mrs. Patterson, Dr. Warren learns that Michael is the product of a normal pregnancy. Birth was uneventful except for a high forceps delivery. Mrs. Patterson describes Michael as being a quiet baby, making few sounds during his first year except for crying. Michael's father took a class in auto mechanics during the baby's first year, found it difficult to study, and was agitated by Michael's crying. To keep her husband, a sometimes violent man, from punishing Michael, Mrs. Patterson quieted the baby. Sometimes, she went so far as to put Michael's crib pillow over his mouth to muffle his sounds.

When he was one year old, Michael said his first word, "hot." Just a few days later he fell on a floor furnace at home burning his hands and legs. He suddenly stopped talking after that and couldn't be coaxed into communicating. When Michael turned two, his parents divorced.

With Mrs. Patterson's permission, Dr. Warren contacts the director of Michael's preschool to gather more background information. She tells him that Michael frequently arrives at preschool with dirty hair and clothes, and that a bath and shampoo for him at school have become a daily ritual. While bathing Michael, the staff has noted cuts and bruises on his back and buttocks. When questioned about them, Michael says, "Mama."

The preschool director notes that Michael uses the bathroom during the day, then often soils his pants just when his mother arrives after work to take him home. One day, a staff member whose car was parked near Mrs. Patterson's, saw her drag Michael along the sidewalk to the car when he refused to go with her.

Dr. Warren's testing reveals that Michael functions near his age level in cognitive, motor, and self-help skills. In contrast, his verbal language is severely delayed. After collecting case history data, teacher observations, and test results, Dr. Warren attempts to integrate his information. He searches for the proper label to identify Michael's disorder, as well as for its etiology or cause.

When we eavesdrop on Dr. Warren's inner dialogue, we find it goes like this: Clearly, Michael is language delayed, but is that this child's main problem? And, what about the cause of his problem? Perhaps Michael was brain-injured at birth as a result of the forceps delivery. That could explain why he didn't babble during the first year. Or, could it be that Michael has experienced physical abuse from both parents and has made an unconscious decision never to speak of it? Still another possibility is that after learning the word, "hot," and then falling and burning himself, Michael came to believe that words have magical powers, so that what you say comes true.

Dr. Warren's dilemma of how to define and explain a child's problem occurs everyday for professionals who work with handicapped children. Traditional approaches encourage classifying or labeling children according to type of handicapping condition. The standard educational categories are **mentally retarded, hearing and visually impaired, speech and language disordered, learning disabled, physically handicapped,** and **emotionally disturbed.** Attaching labels like these to children has a way of lulling professionals into a false sense of security by oversimplifying complex human problems.

Because Mrs. Patterson wants to know the cause of Michael's problem, Dr. Warren attempts to backtrack to find a cause and is caught in the trap of believing that there really is one. As Jackson (1981) aptly puts it, "the cause and effect train goes by only once and once past is incapable of being retrieved" (p. 391). Where human beings are concerned, a single causative factor is rarely ever identifiable, and **multiple causation** is the rule (McFarland, 1974; Gray, 1973; Dossey, 1982).

Figure 1-1. The cause and effect train goes by once and cannot be retrieved.

Logical divisions such as categories **do** seem to make problems more manageable, and it can be useful to categorize children for the purpose of educational placement. However, the danger of categories lies in equating a child with a single characteristic. For example, children in a class for the **educably retarded** can be inferred to be like each other only in regard to their intellectual functioning. They will, no doubt, differ from each other in motivation to learn, special abilities, and learning style. When a special education teacher thinks of children in her class as basically alike just because their I.Q.'s are in the same range, the category impairs teaching rather than enhances it. Blocked by a category, a teacher may find it hard to see around the label and get a look at the child.

But, if we choose to give up the search for causes and categories, what will be our framework? What we need is a theory that will

Figure 1-2. Blocked by a category, a teacher may find it hard to see around the label and get a look at the child.

expand our perceptions rather than limit them. As Bohm (1980) emphasizes, "a theory is primarily a form of insight, a way of looking at the world, and not a form of knowledge of how the world is" (p. 4). A useful theory allows for deletions, additions, and corrections as our perceptions change and grow.

The thesis of this text is that General Systems Theory (GST) is an excellent model for the study of children who are handicapped. It is a model of human behavior which emphasizes wholes, not parts, and synthesis rather than analysis. Like most theories, GST allows us to divide the child into hypothetical parts to study. Unlike most, however, it does not require all the king's horses and all the king's men to put the child back together again.

The following is a brief overview of General Systems Theory and suggestions for its application in evaluation and treatment of handicapped children.

GENERAL SYSTEMS THEORY

Ludwig von Bertalanffy, a biologist, began developing his theory of systems in the 1930's. According to Mark Davidson (1983), Bertalanffy "may well be the least known intellectual titan of the twentieth century" (p. 9). Davidson is the author of **Uncommon Sense: The Life and Thought of Ludwig von Bertalanffy (1901-1972)**.

A scientist, Bertalanffy was frustrated with the accepted models of the day which concerned themselves with two-variable problems (one cause and one effect). He observed that many problems in biology, as well as in the rapidly expanding social sciences, were multi-variable, demanding different conceptual tools. Bertalanffy believed there to be more to an individual organism than the external behavior which can be observed and described. He sought a way to make respectable topics, such as goal-seeking, organization, and regulation, ongoing processes within the organism (Bertalanffy, 1962). Some aspects of these internal processes are visible to the observer; others are not.

Gray, Duhl, and Rizzo (1981), editors of a text on systems theory, see the basic value of GST as being its "human orientation, focusing on man as a system ecologically suspended in multiple systems" (p. xxi). Rephrased, this becomes the basis of our text: **The child is ecologically suspended in multiple systems.** So embedded is the child in this environmental matrix that it becomes impossible to separate one from the other.

Use of the systems approach when evaluating handicapped children means that we cannot just focus upon the child to explain a learning problem. A systems perspective demands that we include the child's family, school, and community in our viewfinder. Two terms commonly used to indicate this broader perspective in problem solving are **holistic** and **ecological**.

General Systems Theory seeks to integrate both systems sciences and the disciplinary sciences and provide a new type of science in which humanistic values are a necessary part. While it is true that GST is still in the infancy of its development, we can hardly fault it on this account, because the social sciences, which deal with the study of man, are in their infancy as well.

Boulding (1956) refers to GST as "the skeleton of a science," meaning that it is left up to the individual student to fill in the appropriate meat or subject matter. We will flesh out the bones of GST with information from child growth and development, embryology, genetics, psychology, sociology, and anthropology, as well as from hybrids such as social psychology, psycholinguistics, and human ecology. In short, we may feel free to draw from whatever disciplines relate to the study of the child, so that we may become as knowledgeable as possible about our subject.

Systems theorists have taken on the ambitious project of explaining phenomena of the universe by using parallel theories at all levels of systems. They stress similarities between mathematics, physics, and engineering, often referred to as the **hard sciences**; and psychology, sociology, and anthropology, the **soft sciences**. Systems theorists await the day when, in kinship, the lion will lie down with the lamb.

One of the most important elements of systems theory is the concept of system. Bertalanffy (1956) defines a system as "a set of units with relationships among them" (p. 3). Miller (1978) explains that here the word **set** implies that the units have some common properties: "These common properties are essential if the units are to interact or have relationships. The state of each unit is constrained by, conditioned by, or dependent on the state of other units" (p. 16).

Davidson (1983) clarifies these definitions of system by this description: "A system is a manifestation of something intangible, but quite real, called organization. A system, like a work of art, is a pattern rather than a pile. Like a piece of music, it's an arrangement rather than an aggregate. Like a marriage, it's a relationship rather than an encounter" (p. 27). Key words to remember in regard to a system are **organization** and **relationship**.

In studying the child, we employ a **living system** model. Living systems are a subset of all systems and function on a number of levels, from the simplest one-celled organism to the incredibly complex society of nations. Table I shows how these levels of system relate to our study of the child.

Living systems have both subsystems, or parts, and suprasystems,

Table 1-I
LEVELS OF LIVING SYSTEMS

Increasing Complexity ↑		
	Society of Nations	
	Society	COMMUNITY
	Organization	SCHOOL
	Group	FAMILY
	Organism	CHILD
	Organ	
	Cell	

wholes of which they are a part. As an example, the heart is a subsystem of the human body, which is its suprasystem. The individual is dependent upon the heart's functioning for life, and, likewise, the heart has no life of its own without the body to sustain it.

Just as we speak of hard and soft sciences, we refer to hard and soft definitions of a system. As Rapaport (1970) explains, a hard definition permits an exacting explanation of the thing under study and implies a mathematical model and predictive power. Hard definitions are put to use in the physical sciences and in engineering; for example, in studying rocks, planets, or clocks.

While human behavior lends itself to methodological study, it is by far too complex for mathematical quantification or for computer modeling. Even in what might appear to be simple human situations, a myriad of variables are operating.

Soft theories, according to Rapaport, are characterized by "explanatory appeal." The soft definition of a system is this: "a portion of the world that is perceived as a unit and that is able to maintain its 'identity' in spite of changes going on in it" (p. 22). A soft definition would be employed in studying the child as a system, or a human group such as a family, a Sunday school class, or a public school. Human groups are referred to as **social systems.**

While there is no clear boundary to a social system such as a family (in contrast to another living system like an amoeba or a fox), a family, nonetheless, maintains its identity. The Honeycutts are as much a family when Dad goes to the plant, Mom to her office job, and the children to school, as when they are in close proximity, seated around the dining table for breakfast.

According to Parsons (1959), the role, rather than the individual, is the smallest unit of a social system. The definition of role is "the expected behavior of an individual in a group" (Sherif and Sherif, 1956, p. 18). Families are made up of roles such as mother, father, daughter, and brother. Individual family members play one or more roles. Mrs. Honeycutt, for example, is both wife and mother in her family; Jeremiah, age 10, is son and brother.

In this day of changing lifestyles, it is sometimes difficult to say what constitutes a family. Are single parents with children families? How do we classify a person who chooses to live alone, or individuals who live together, but who are not married. When we employ the definition of system as our definition of family, we see that all of these ways of living qualify as family life. That is, all of these families represent a portion of the world perceived as a unit and able to maintain its identity despite changes inside or outside system boundaries.

Returning to the Honeycutt family, we see that they do not cease being a family when changes occur from within. Divorce, death of a family member, remarriage, children leaving home— none of these turn of events appreciably affect the integrity of the Honeycutts as a family.

When we say a child is in a family, it is understood to mean that only part of his or her identity comes from the family. An individual is never entirely absorbed within family boundaries, because there is a psychological system which remains separate.

The psychological self is that part of the child which exists beyond the roles that are played. Children take on roles in a variety of systems. For example, Samantha, age 7, is a daughter and sister in her family system, and a friend and student in her classroom system. Those closest to her know that there is a Samantha untouched by these roles. Her mother noted that Samantha had a personality all her own when she brought her home that first day from the hospital.

Samantha was a friendlier baby than her brothers Jeremiah and Joshua had been; she was more eager to explore, and she had a higher level of energy. Mrs. Honeycutt, having only one daughter,

Figure 1-3. Samantha takes on a number of roles within the Honeycutt family.

was eager to teach her little girl to cook and sew, but Samantha showed personal preferences for playing outdoors, learning to hit a softball, and being called "Sam." When she grows up, Sam says she wants to be an airplane pilot. What Mother sometimes thinks of as stubbornness is actually Samantha's psychological self. While influenced by role requirements, the psychological self ultimately maintains its separateness from them.

Just as the child is a subsystem of the family, the family is a subsystem of the community; the community of the state; the state of the nation; and the nation of the international community. Obviously, it would be an endless, and fruitless, task to describe all the systems which in some way affect a child. In outlining the boundary of a problem, our concern is those systems which have the greatest impact upon a child's life and learning experiences, and which have the most potential for change.

All living systems (from cell to society) share certain characteristics which we shall refer to again and again in our discussion of the child as a system. These are **input, throughput, output, feedback, vital balance,** and **system distress.**

Input-Throughput-Output

A living system is referred to as **open** because it maintains an open-arms stance in relation to its environment. This means that living systems readily permit inputs of matter-energy and information to cross their boundaries. Matter-energy inputs activate the physiological functioning of the organism's **biological system.** Living systems require sufficient amounts of heat, light, food, and water for survival.

For human beings and human groups, specific patterns of information input are equally important for system survival. Information in the form of auditory, visual, and tactile stimuli is critical to the physiological and psychological functioning of a child. Infants whose environments do not provide adequate input in the form of talking, hugging, rocking, and playing can fail to thrive and, in extreme cases, die.

The child lucky enough to be born into a family environment rich with auditory, visual, and tactile stimuli takes in the information, or **input,** and, in turn, reflects it in verbal and nonverbal ways as **output.** Information processes within a system as **throughput.** Thinking, imagining, and evaluating are examples of a child's throughput. While we cannot observe throughput directly, we can infer that it exists. For example, a child speaks, and we infer thinking; composes a poem, and we infer creativity; completes a task, and we infer motivation.

Each child sets out on the adventure into learning with hereditary inputs which tend to foster or deter the learning process. From the very beginning of their lives, children differ in regard to intelligence, sensory capabilities, learning style, and motivation to learn. The **genetic template** is the blueprint or program for a child. Miller (1978) defines the genetic template as "the original information input that is the program for its later structure and process, which can be modified by later matter-energy or information inputs from its environment" (p. 34).

A child's template defines certain limits; for example, eyes cannot be both blue and brown. The template also establishes ranges of possibilities, as in the area of intelligence. What a child's I.Q. will be at age eight is not set in the template, but rather a range of intelligence (superior, average, retarded) is established. Environmental inputs in the form of information can move a child along this invisible continuum, as, for example, from low average to high average intelligence.

Information is channeled between individuals and between groups by means of communication lines. Examples of lines which link systems are messages left by family members for each other on a kitchen blackboard, memos from principal to teachers and back again in a school system, and telephone wires within a community. The more lines of communication there are within a system, the more tightly bound the system, and the more energized it becomes.

Feedback

The study of the control mechanisms a system employs is called **cybernetics**. The feedback loop is the basic mechanism for the control of a system. Specifically, feedback refers to a communications network which produces action in response to an input of information. Of the two major kinds of feedback loops, one is the type which is wholly internal to a system, involving closed loops which do not cross the boundary of a system, and which is called **internal feedback**.

An example of internal feedback, at the level of organism, would be temperature regulation within the human body. Another example, this time at the level of group, would be Ms. Sylvester's adjusting the thermostat to warm up her classroom because the children complain of being cold. In both cases, all activity is internal to the system.

Now let's imagine that instead of adjusting the thermostat, Ms. Sylvester goes to the principal's office inquiring as to whether or not the rest of the building is cold. She discovers that the heat has gone off. She returns to her class, quickly shuts out all drafts, and tells the children to get their coats from their lockers. This is an example of the second type of feedback in operation, **external feedback**.

In external feedback, the feedback path exits through the output boundary (Ms. Sylvester leaves the classroom), passes through the environment where the information is modified (she goes to the principal's office and discovers that the heat is off), and re-enters at the input boundary, the rest of the loop being completed within the system (she returns and tells the children to bundle up).

Internal feedback acts as a maintenance man keeping all subsystems functioning. External feedback is disciplinarian, encouraging the system to reach its goals and shooing it back on course when it strays. Through the interplay of internal and external feedback, a system strikes a balance among its subsystems and with its suprasystem and environment.

We speak of feedback as being positive, maintaining the growth and survival of the system, or negative, supplying information that the system is off course or out of bounds. When Ms. Sylvester's fourth graders complete a math assignment, her feedback to them may be positive, "You guys did great; you've all learned your multiplication tables," or negative, "There's still confusion over times; let's do one more assignment on multiplication for tomorrow." Negative, in systems terms, is not synonymous with critical. Ms. Sylvester's negative feedback merely lets the children know that they are off course in pursuit of their goal of mastering multiplication.

Vital Balance

As we have seen, living systems at all levels tend to maintain an orderly balance, both among their subsystems and with their environment. This balance is referred to as homeostasis and is achieved by a complex network of feedback loops. While the homeostatic model explains many aspects of human behavior, it is not sufficient to explain all its varieties. Allport (1961) describes homeostasis as a "stay-put" concept. "It is static, unprogressive, allowing inadequately for either change or growth. The picture is one of a semiclosed system, not of a system fully open to the world, capable of expanding and becoming more than it is" (p. 89).

The model fails to explain the spontaneous activities of living systems and the processes of growth, development, and creation

(Bertalanffy, 1981). Granted, many of a child's observed behaviors involve response to outside stimulation and relief from tension. However, once a child's basic needs for food, physical comfort, and safety are met, another set of equally-strong needs comes into play — to create, risk, and stretch to the limit of one's abilities.

As Allport explains: "New experiences, which most of us crave, cannot be put in terms of tension-reduction, nor can our desire to acquire knowledge for its own sake, to create works of beauty and usefulness, nor to give and receive love, for love involves all manner of responsibilities and strains" (p. 90).

Menninger, Mayman, and Pruyser (1963) refer to the dynamic interactions of individual and environment as a "vital balance." This term encompasses the tension-reducing and the tension-producing qualities of human beings. Healthy children maintain a vital balance with their environment by sometimes putting themselves in situations which invite stress. For example, a first-grade boy with a stuttering problem volunteers for show-and-tell, putting himself under self-imposed pressure to communicate. One of his classmates, a little girl who has a fear of water, asks to enroll for a class in water safety. In the case of both children, their goal is clearly the production of tension ultimately leading to personal growth. As these children demonstrate, a vital balance involves not just maintaining the status quo, but, sometimes, upsetting the apple cart.

System Distress

An unexpected external disturbance stresses a system, producing internal strain. After a system upset, feedback circuits strive to return the system to its predisturbance state. Sometimes this is possible, sometimes it is not. The overall effect of any disturbance upon a system is determined by the system's internal and external resources available to counterbalance it. A child psychiatrist in the Midwest was diagnosed as learning-disabled when he was seven. As he describes it, the pages in his reader played tricks on him as the b's flipflopped into d's and back again. He was able to ground himself by saying outloud, "b's have bellies, d's don't." Other learning-disabled children in his class, lacking such a cheerful coping technique, fell steadily behind in reading, some eventually dropping out of school.

Miller (1981) explains that all adjustment processes on the part of a system entail certain costs. These costs are in the form of energy, material resources, time, and information. Social systems rely on a special form of information conveyed on a marker of metal or paper and referred to as money. When resources of time, money, and professionals are in short supply, a child may be unable to stabilize following a major system disturbance.

Compare the outcomes of two seven-year-old boys, Ron and Chris, who have cerebral palsy. Both have normal intelligence, and both have moderate physical impairment. Ron lives in a small rural community and is the only physically-handicapped child in his school system. The community does not have a hospital, and the only special education class in the school is for the mentally retarded. Chris lives in a city where physical and occupational therapy are readily available. A developmental psychologist sees Chris yearly for evaluation and plans a specialized school program for him. He is mainstreamed for most classes and attends learning lab for reading. By fourth grade, Ron is scoring in the 80–90 range on intellectual testing, and his school work is at second-grade level. Chris continues to test in the average range of intelligence and scores at grade level in math, reading, and spelling.

Regardless of resources available, however, some types of distress are devastating to a system, overwhelming the regulatory circuits. Some of these types of distress are mental retardation, autism, and terminal illness.

Because of the complex nature of a system and the interdependence of its parts, a disturbance in one subsystem will eventually affect other subsystems. Imagine for a moment a group of balloons, with their strings tied together. A gust of wind touches one balloon and it begins to bob. It, in turn, nudges its neighbor, which touches two more, and soon all are moving. The balloons are like the systems of a child. By the time a child is seen for evaluation, what began as an isolated disturbance in one system may now have produced an effect upon the whole. When we see a handicapped child, the learning problem to be defined is not bounded by the child. Viewing the child and environment as one, we look at all systems, enlarging the boundary of the problem to include the child, family, school, and community.

As we view children from a systems perspective, it is important to keep in mind:

- The child is composed of biological and psychological subsystems and is, in turn, a component of family, school, and community suprasystems.
- The child is a system ecologically suspended in multiple systems, so that it is impossible to separate child from environment.
- A genetic template in combination with environmental inputs determine a child's potential for learning.
- Inputs to the child-system are processed as throughput and reflected in observable performance or output.
- Regulatory mechanisms help protect the child from external disturbance.
- A vital balance exists between relaxation from tension and tension production within the child, and this balance is critical for survival and growth.

* * * * * *

In Chapter 2, we will examine the evaluation process.

Chapter 2

THE ECOLOGY OF EVALUATION

Michael Patterson's kindergarten teacher will, no doubt, rely heavily on Dr. Warren's final report as she plans an educational program for Michael. She will probably skim the pages of the report looking for a diagnosis and then skip from there to recommendations.

A report written in systems style does not culminate in a diagnosis. Rather than classify a child or uncover the cause of a child's handicap, the goals of a systems evaluation are to:

- Determine which system of the child (biological, psychological, or social) is the primary system disturbed. **Primary** here means both first in **importance** (the system most disturbed) and first in **time** (the system where the disturbance originated).
- Estimate the relative influence of template and environment upon learning.
- Describe the child's individual learning style.
- List the steps to be taken to encourage well-being at all levels of system.

Table 2-I
GOALS OF A SYSTEMS EVALUATION

- Determine which system of the child (biological, psychological, or social) is the primary system disturbed. **Primary** here means both first in **importance** (the system most disturbed) and first in **time** (the system where the disturbance originated).
- Estimate the relative influence of template and environment upon learning.
- Describe the child's individual learning style.
- List the steps to be taken to encourage well-being at all levels of system.

Educational treatment is a high priority for handicapped children. In this chapter, we will explore the ways children learn and the

20

ways handicapping conditions can disrupt the learning process. Next, we will look at the steps in evaluation, and, finally, using Michael Patterson as an example, we will put the systems approach into action.

WAYS CHILDREN LEARN

As we discovered in Chapter 1, every newborn enters the world with certain traits programmed into the genetic template. Inborn ranges of ability are preset in the areas of intelligence, sensory capabilities, capacity for the storage of memories, style of learning, and motivation to learn. Environmental variables, as varied as protein intake, parent-child bonds, and time spent in play interact with genetic variables to produce the child seen at evaluation. Even then, modifications of a child's environment promise further possibilities for change.

Figure 2-1. Traits and ranges of ability which affect the learning process are programmed into the child's template.

Three distinct communication bands bear information from environment to baby. The three types of information conveyed along these bands are sounds, sights, and sensations. These are referred to as **auditory, visual,** and **tactile** stimuli, respectively, and are received by highly specialized receptors in a baby's ears, eyes, and skin.

Infants crave the information the world has to offer. Stern (1977) stresses that "the infant, from birth, will seek out stimulation and even work for it. In fact, the seeking of stimulation has by now achieved the status of a drive or motivational tendency not unlike that of hunger" (p. 52).

Depending upon the status of a newborn's senses, certain kinds of information may be utilized effectively by baby and others may not. For example, a baby who is blind at birth joins the world prepared to take in its sounds and sensations but not its sights. A baby born deaf can receive environmental sights and sensations but not sounds.

When no handicapping condition is present, most babies readily take in all three types of information. The baby girl who is staring into Daddy's eyes as she is sung to and rocked is being bombarded by all three types of input simultaneously. Human contact conveniently provides all types of critical stimuli—auditory, visual, and tactile. Nature itself is a school for babies, offering an incredible array of noises, colors, and textures. People-made objects are also good sources of stimuli—records for listening, paper birds suspended over a crib for looking, a teddy bear for holding.

A factor which controls a baby's utilization of information is **attending,** which involves readying oneself to take in information. In order to take in sounds from the environment, a baby must have the ability to hear, but also must be **ready** to listen. To take in sights, he or she must be **ready** to look, and to take in sensations, **ready** to reach out and touch. The words, **listening, looking,** and **touching,** imply a child's active participation in the learning process. Attending goes beyond the **ability** to take in information and reflects the readiness and willingness to do so.

The behaviors in an infant or child which signal a readiness to learn are subtle compared to the readying behavior of animals. It is easy to tell when something catches the attention of a dog, for

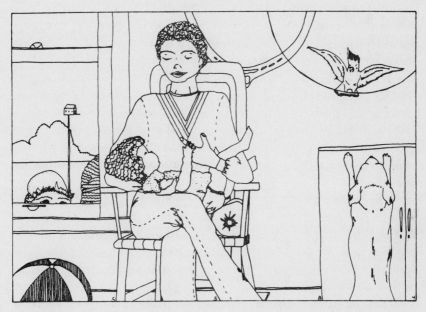

Figure 2-2. Visual, auditory, and tactile stimuli bombard a child simultaneously.

example. When a dog spots a squirrel in a tree, its ears perk up, its muscles stiffen, and its tail wags. The clues a baby gives that he or she is attending are much more subtle—a slight turn of the head, a widening of the eyes, a mild tensing of the body.

We know that the way to get and hold the attention of a living system is by manipulating the quality and quantity of information available within the environment. All levels of living systems prefer inputs which are intense, spatially extensive, moving, changing, repeated a few times, and colorful—in other words, complex and high in informational content. As Miller (1978) explains: "Decreased rates of information input lower the degrees of arousal and attention. Monotonous inputs repeated many times have the same effect" (p. 428). This means that a baby seeks intense levels of stimulation and craves changes—a new crib toy, a new lullaby—from time to time. Jantsch (1981) adds that in regard to systems: "Total novelty means chaos, total confirmation equilibrium and death" (p. 98). So it is important to strike a balance between environmental sameness and newness.

Input to the child-system exits in the form of output, a type of observable behavior. In regard to learning, the three main input-output channels are **listening-speaking** (language skills), **looking-acting** (fine and gross motor skills), and **touching-interacting** (gross motor and social skills). Children who utilize primarily the listening-speaking channel favor **auditory** input; the looking-acting channel, **visual** input; and the touching-interacting channel, **tactile** input.

The learning process, of course, is much more complex than this model would suggest, because all three input-output channels overlap one another. A fifth-grade girl taking an oral spelling quiz watches and listens carefully as her teacher pronounces the spelling word. The student then responds by spelling the word aloud. The input channels the girl is utilizing are **listening** and **looking**; the output channels are **speaking** and **interacting**. If the spelling test is written, the student prints the word after it is spoken by her teacher. This process involves **listening/looking**, followed by **acting**.

When one input-output channel is unavailable to a child because of a handicapping condition, another channel can take its place, although the substitute channel is usually not as efficient as the primary one for that sensory activity. As an example, the primary mode of communication in hearing individuals is the **listening-speaking** channel. In place of listening-speaking, a hearing-impaired child may substitute **listening/looking-speaking** (lipreading and speaking) as a means of communication; a deaf child may employ **looking-acting** (lipreading and signing).

Even when the ability to take in information in all three input channels and the readiness to do so are present, most children still tend to favor one input channel over the others. As one type of input gains in favor with a baby, options are lost and learning patterns are set.

After years of screening out certain types of input in favor of others, by preschool age, children may already be stuck in a favored way of perceiving. Several years later, when they enter school, this fact may pose problems for teachers who must teach language to a child who favors visual information or teach art to a child who prefers auditory input.

Preferences in regard to different bands of information can be observed in the crib. These differences tend to fall along sex lines. According to Restak (1979), recent psychobiological research indicates that many of the differences in learning style between the sexes are "innate, biologically determined, and relatively resistant to change through the influences of culture" (p. 197). This means that preferences in regard to learning style are programmed into the genetic template.

Male and Female Differences

Restak (1979) reviewed hundreds of current research projects relating to male and female differences in learning style. In comparison to boys, the girls tested were found to be:

- More sensitive to sounds, especially their mother's voice.
- More proficient at fine motor performance.
- More attentive to social contexts, meaning faces, speech patterns, tones of voice.
- Able to speak sooner and possess larger vocabularies.

Compared to the girls, the boys were found to:

- Demonstrate early superiority in visual acuity.
- Be more clumsy.
- Perform poorly in fine motor movements, but better in gross total body movements.
- Possess better spatial abilities, dealing better with three-dimensional space.

An oversimplification of the findings would be to say that boys tend to be **visual learners,** and that girls tend to be **auditory learners;** but, as usual, when it comes to human beings, the situation is far more complex than this. Each child appears to possess his or her own **unique** style of learning. Some children rely primarily on one input channel, others prefer two of the three channels, still others utilize all three to varying degrees.

To understand how these styles of learning come to life in children, let's take a look at children who represent the three basic styles of learning.

The Looker

As a baby, it is apparent that Lyle prefers the **looking-acting** mode of learning. In the first few months of his life, Lyle's mother notes that he is visually active, searching his room for objects to look at. He can be quieted by his mother's face or by another visual stimulus such as the movement of his crib mobile.

As a toddler, Lyle likes picture books, preferring to turn the pages and take in the pictures rather than listen to the accompanying story. By two and a half, Lyle has learned the primary colors. When traveling in the car with his parents, he looks attentively at passing billboards and scenery. He often points out details in the scenery that would have been missed by his parents, such as a cow in a distant field—"Look, mama, cow."

By four, Lyle is playing with his dad's pocket calculator, pushing the buttons and watching the numbers come and go. He learns his numbers long before he recognizes the letters of the alphabet and starts drawing almost as soon as he can hold a pencil. By the time he reaches school age, he is putting model cars and airplanes together with the help of his dad and a diagram; later, a diagram alone will suffice.

In the first grade, Lyle learns to spell words by printing them and quickly masters a sight word vocabulary. Phonics comes a bit slower, until he figures out how to pair alphabet letters with sounds, catching onto the fact that two letters sometimes make just one sound, as in **sh**. Lyle is fascinated by hand-held electronic games, television shows, and movies. He likes checkers and Concentration; later, Scrabble and chess. (We will be reacquainted with Lyle in later chapters.)

The Listener

Lyle's cousin, Madeleine, prefers the **listening-speaking** mode of learning. As an infant, when distressed, she can be quieted by the sound of a familiar voice or of her music box. Madeleine likes being talked to when taking a bottle, even though the words do not yet have meaning. She likes picture books as did Lyle, but she likes the story better than the pictures, sometimes closing her eyes and leaning against her father while he reads to her.

Madeleine learns her ABC song long before kindergarten and entertains herself by talking to her dolls and by listening to music on her portable cassette player which she takes with her on trips in the car.

In first grade she learns phonics quickly and reads easily, attacking new words with confidence. Madeleine enjoys her role as teacher's pet. She listens well to directions, and she doesn't have to be told what to do over again as do many of the little boys in her first-grade class. She learns spelling words by spelling them aloud to herself. Madeleine excels at listening games like "Simon Says." She can put together a model plane or sew a potholder on her toy sewing machine but only when the directions are read aloud to her as she follows.

The Mover

Madeleine's brother, Carl, prefers the **touching-interacting** mode of learning. As a baby, he can be quieted only if he is picked up and held, touch being his favored medium of communication. As a toddler, he can't seem to sit still for story time, preferring instead to be outside at play in his sandbox.

Carl quickly learns to ride a tricycle, and once on it in the morning, he can hardly be coaxed off for meal times. In his preschool years, Carl continues to seek out body contact and likes to be rocked by his mother and held on a lap much longer than did his sister, Madeleine. During trips in the car, Carl fidgets in the backseat, sometimes succeeding in starting a fight with Madeleine.

When Carl puts together models, he does so by touch alone, not needing directions or a diagram. He likes all types of crafts and outdoor sports, excelling at softball and soccer. Spelling and reading do not come easily for Carl as they do for the **listeners** and **lookers** in his first-grade class. By second grade, an observant teacher has noted his lags in academic areas and sends him to a tutor for after-school help. Carl's third-grade teacher is pleased to discover that he is one of the few boys in her class who can square dance, coordinating hand and foot movements with music.

These three learning styles reflect differences in cerebral development and organization. To understand the ways children learn, it is critical to have some understanding of the functioning of the organ in charge of the learning process—the human brain.

The Brain

The **neuron** is the basic unit of structure of the brain. The wrinkled, pinkish-gray outer surface of the brain is called the cortex, and it contains billions of neurons and the axons that connect them to each other. Inputs of information to a neuron are by way of a number of branching **dendrites**, and output is by way of a single **axon**. The region of communication between the axon of one neuron and the dendrite of another is called a **synapse**.

Axons are covered with a specialized myelin sheath of white fatty tissue. Teyler (1978) explains that the functions of the myelin sheath are to "insulate the axon from its immediate surroundings and to speed its message-transmitting capacity by a factor of 10 or so" (p. 10). The process of myelinization is not complete at birth. In fact, the brain regions related to language do not myelinate until about age five; some other regions not until puberty.

The human brain is bilaterally symmetrical. The two identical-appearing hemispheres are bound to each other by the **corpus callosum**, the largest fiber tract in the brain. The corpus callosum contains over 200 million neurons that interconnect the left and right hemispheres.

We know that a child's range of intellectual ability is contained within the genetic template. According to Bouchard (1976), 75 to 80 percent of intellectual functioning is due to innate or heritable causes. He adds, however, that environmental stimuli can produce an important biological effect on the child. And, Gould (1981) states flatly that it is a fallacy to equate "heritable" with "inevitable."

To determine the actual effects of environment on brain development, Walsh (1981) studied two groups of rats from the same litter. One group was raised in an enriched environment consisting of a large cage which had a changing selection of objects such as ladders, wheels, light bulbs, and tunnels. The other group had smaller cages. They were kept either in isolation or in small groups with solid metal walls between them, so that they couldn't see or touch the other rats. The rats were kept in their respective environments for periods of 30 to 80 days, and then their brains were analyzed for anatomical and biochemical changes that might have occurred.

When compared with the other group, the rats from enriched environments had: Increased brain weight, especially in the frontal cortex; increased brain size, mostly in cerebral length; and, enlargement of cortical neurons, with an increase in both number and relative area of synapses. Walsh concludes: "It is clear that the structure and function of the brain can no longer be considered in isolation from its environment" (p. 153). In other words, the brain actively adapts its structures and functions in response to auditory, visual, and tactile input.

The Two Sides of the Brain

Information entering a child-system via the three primary input channels is processed directly by the brain. The two sides of the brain control opposite sides of the body; the left side of the brain controlling the right side of the body, and the right side of the brain controlling the left side of the body.

In most people, the left hemisphere of the brain is specialized for the storage of language, and the right hemisphere for the storage of images and impressions. A number of terms have been used to show the different thinking styles of the two sides of the brain. Terms for left hemisphere thinking are **analytic, causal, intellectual, sequential**; for right hemisphere thinking, **creative, holistic, intuitive, synthetic.**

Samples (1976) refers to the right hemisphere as the "metaphoric mind." A metaphor is a figure of speech which links one thing to another by comparison, such as "He is a bear in the morning." According to Samples, the role of metaphoric thinking is "to invent, to create, and to challenge conformity by extending what is known into new meadows of knowing. The metaphoric mind treats all input as fragments of reality, and as soon as a fragment appears the mind begins the search for the whole" (p. 19). The right hemisphere is a master of this type of inventive, holistic thinking.

Ornstein (1977) was one of the first brain researchers to bring to the attention of the public the roles of the two hemispheres and to stress the underutilization of the right hemisphere. In the first edition of his book, **The Psychology of Consciousness**, published in 1970, he suggested that those of us who live in the Western world may be using only half of our brain potential. The academic subjects stressed in school—reading, spelling, arithmetic—are almost exclusively left hemisphere abilities. Those who succeed in tapping right brain abilities are creative individuals such as musicians, poets, and inventors (Edwards, 1979; Virshup, 1978).

While the dichotomy between the two hemispheres is fascinating, it is misleading to think that in all people these are clear-cut distinctions. Gazzaniga and LeDoux (1978) speak of "right half-brain" and "left half-brain" to emphasize that, except in extreme cases where one hemisphere is missing because of injury or surgery, the two half-brains function as a whole. They are able to operate as one because of the integrative role of the corpus callosum.

Recall that the interhemispheric connections, especially the fibers innervating the language areas, do not fully myelinate until about age five. Until then, each side of the brain could be storing **engrams**, or traces of language, virtually unaware of what is going on in the other hemisphere. If there is damage fo a child's left hemisphere prior to age five, the right hemisphere is capable of taking over control of linguistic development. The sole control by one hemisphere of a specific ability is referred to as **lateralization**.

It is possible then that linguistic mechanisms may emerge bilaterally during early development and only later consolidate in the left hemisphere. Perhaps the left half-brain matures first and so gains control of language and motor development. For now, the determining factor in lateralization or lack of it is not clear; however, we do know that there are a number of ways that the two types of thinking can be represented in the brain without posing problems to the learner.

For example, 95 percent of right handers have **language** lateralized to the left hemisphere and the **metaphoric mind** to the right hemisphere. The other five percent of right handers have **language** lateralized to the right hemisphere (**metaphoric mind** to the left) or have a bilateral representation of the two types of thinking.

In regard to left handers, 70 percent have **language** in the left hemisphere and the **metaphoric mind** in the right. Fifteen percent of left handers have **language** in the right hemisphere (**metaphoric mind** in the left), and the remaining 15 percent have bilateral representation of the two types of thinking.

Blakeslee (1980) offers an appealing explanation for the complete lateralization of language in some people and bilateral representation in others. He describes the extreme case of lateralization (**language** solely in one hemisphere, **metaphoric mind** in the other) as a "partnership of two narrow specialists: One is adept at verbal and logical thinking while the other is specialized for nonverbal, holistic thinking." The opposite extreme (speech and metaphor distributed throughout both hemispheres) is more like a "partnership of two generalists: Each is equally adept at any kind of problem, so the partners can help one another and check each other's work for errors" (p. 100).

So rather than draw lines of distinction between the two hemispheres, it seems more fruitful to distinguish between the two basic types of ability present in the human brain. One is the ability to speak, to think logically and to see cause and effect relationships; the other is the ability to see the whole, mediate by metaphor, and be creative. Exactly where each of the two types of ability resides within the brain is a highly individual matter.

As we shall see, the systems perspective allows us to make use of both types of thinking in our evaluations of children. We will be thinking **analytically** when we look at children's development in a sequential, orderly way; and **holistically** as we integrate biological, psychological, and social systems of a child. Now, let's turn our attention to the evaluation process.

THE EVALUATION PROCESS

There are two distinct parts to an evaluation. The first is the case history, and the second is observation and testing.

The Case History, or "This Is Your Life!"

The case history is usually taken before testing is begun. It is a detailed account of a child's life to date as recalled by family members and includes questions about pregnancy and birth, about the child's developmental, nutritional, medical, and educational history, and about the family constellation.

In taking a case history, it is important to keep in mind the fallibility of parents' memories. When recalling the past, it is human nature to sift memories through a sieve, screening out ones that are painful. Some parents may bring their baby book to the initial interview, but this is still no guarantee that the information written down is factual. Did Sara truly say her first word at seven months as recorded, or was she stringing together sounds in play and a first-time mother heard, "mama?"

Some parents may have no written records, yet are able to recall a multitude of details, painting a vivid picture of their child's early life. When there are a number of children in the family, the best the parents may be able to do is compare the child to be evaluated with siblings of the same sex: "Did Owen walk at about the same age as your older son, John? Was he toilet trained earlier or later?"

In the case history interview, we do not attempt to peer down the tracks of the past in search of the cause and effect train. Instead, our purpose is to discover which system (or systems) of the child is experiencing the greatest disturbance. As we shall see, this information is the basis for determining the severity of a problem and appropriate treatment.

Now, let's return to Michael Patterson, this time looking from a systems perspective at the information gathered by Dr. Warren. When Dr. Warren asked Mrs. Patterson about her pregnancy, Michael's birth and early development, he was in fact exploring the integrity of Michael's biological system. High forceps delivery and marked delay in language acquisition point to early disturbance within the biological system. (Later chapters in this book contain detailed histories of biological, psychological, and social systems.) Dr. Warren is investigating the health of the psychological system when he asks about Michael's first word, his personality as a baby, and his relationship with his mother. Matters of concern in Michael's case are: His first word was "hot" rather than "mama" or "dada"; he began talking and apparently decided to stop; Mrs. Patterson relates to Michael in a punitive way; and toileting problems persist. This combination of factors points to a disturbance within the psychological system. Michael's marked delay in language skills must eventually disrupt relationships with peers and adults. Dr. Warren's observations of Michael will shed light upon the integrity of the social system.

Observation and Testing

Observation and testing usually follow the case history interview. Teachers and parents who are unfamiliar with testing procedures may imagine that in some magical way a child can be revealed to them in a three-page report. The written results of an evaluation, however, do not mean that this is all there is to know about a child; they mean only that this is all the child has permitted us to see.

Remember the role is the expected behavior of an individual in a social situation. A child who has not been tested before will be unclear about how one is expected to act in the presence of a stranger with a briefcase and stopwatch. Parents and teachers rarely prepare children for testing by explaining how to play the role of a child being tested. In response to unclear expectations or expectations which make it difficult to conform (sit still, pay attention, talk on command), a child may withdraw, exposing very little of himself or herself in the testing role.

Testing very young children (preschool age and under) involves other special problems. Young children warm up more slowly to a testing situation than do school-age children, tire more quickly, and are less verbal. The evaluator of a preschool child may begin testing at a table and end up on the floor, in a sandbox, or on a merry-go-round. Mauser (1977) and Darley (1979) present lists of test instruments for use in evaluating preschool and school-age children.

Michael Patterson spent the first fifteen minutes of his testing session hiding behind the couch in Dr. Warren's office. Ignoring Michael, Dr. Warren proceeded to build a spaceship with Tinkertoys, and a few minutes later Michael ventured out to watch. Michael looked carefully at all the toys in the room, spotted a clown on a top shelf, pulled on Dr. Warren's coattail, and pointed to the clown. While Michael spoke many times during the hour and a half session, he relied on the same few stock utterances, "Where Mama?" "my home," and "no."

During the testing at a small, preschool-size table, Michael repeatedly jumped up and out of his seat. Dr. Warren had to constantly direct Michael's attention back to the test items. Michael did not listen well, often beginning a test item before directions were complete. Michael resisted being touched, slinking away when Dr. Warren reached out to pat him on the back at the completion of testing. Michael also refused a piece of gum offered to him. The test data revealed Michael to be functioning at age level in cognitive, motor, and self-help skills. Only one of the skills tested was dramatically deficient — expressive language.

We now have most of the needed information at hand to complete a systems evaluation of Michael. Our intent is to:

- **Determine which system of the child is the primary system disturbed.** In Michael's case, biological, psychological, and social systems seem equally disturbed.
- **Estimate the relative influence of template and environment upon learning.** Michael's history suggests inborn learning problems coupled not only with lack of rewards, but perhaps punishment by his mother for expression.
- **Describe individual learning style.** Test results and personal observations indicate that Michael tunes out auditory and tactile stimuli, preferring visual information.
- **List the steps to be taken to encourage wellbeing at all levels of system.** To answer this question we have to look at the treatment process.

TREATMENT

While evaluation may reveal a child's disturbance to be primarily at the biological level, to be ecological, treatment must be geared to all levels of system. There are two basic types of treatment. These are: **Process**-oriented therapy, which readies a child to learn, and **content**-oriented therapy, which provides specific communication, motor, self-help, interpersonal, and academic skills to be learned. Process refers to **how** one learns; content, to **what** is learned.

Table 2-II

**EXAMPLES OF PROFESSIONALS WHO PROVIDE TREATMENT TO HANDICAPPED
CHILDREN AND THEIR ORIENTATION TO TREATMENT**

Process	Process-Content	Content
Audiologist	Dance therapist	Occupational therapist
Neonatologist	Nutritionist	Learning disability teacher
Pediatric neurologist	Physical therapist	Special education teacher
Otolaryngologist	Psychologist	Teacher of the blind
Pediatrician	Speech-language pathologist	Teacher of the deaf

It is extremely important for there to be a **master plan** of treatment for a handicapped child, ideally with one professional acting as coordinator. The coordinator may be a physician, psychologist, speech-language pathologist, or other health care professional. His or her role is to see that all appropriate referrals are made and to keep the family informed about community resources. All professionals who work with handicapped children should consider keeping a resource file to be an important part of their work. That way, regardless of where a child enters the health care system, referrals to all needed services will be available.

Just as families tend to look for single causes for their child's problem, they tend to search for single solutions. But, as we know, even when one system of a child is disturbed, the balance of all systems will be upset, so that treatment is usually required at more than one level of system.

As a rule, professionals who provide services to handicapped children tend to focus on either learning **process** or **content**. As an example, let's say a five-year-old boy who has a learning disability is referred to an optometrist because he squints when he reads and frequently loses his place. The optometrist fits the boy with glasses for desk work, and, in this way, readies the child for the intake of information, the **process** of learning. In contrast, the boy's learning disability teacher stresses the visual recall of letters, sight words, and numbers, the **content** of learning.

A psychologist is an example of a professional who may play either or both treatment roles. A psychologist might help to prepare a child to learn by lowering defenses and lessening fears in regard to learning (**process**) or might teach a child specific social skills to aid in forming relationships with peers and teachers (**content**). (The glossary contains a list of health care professionals and their roles in treatment. Table III gives examples of process- and content-oriented therapy.)

The services of at least three specialists will be needed to help Michael Patternson. A referral should be made to a **pediatric neurologist** to examine Michael for possible brain injury (biological system), to a **clinical psychologist** to help mend the mother-child relationship (psychological system), and to a **speech-language pathologist** to improve Michael's communication skills (social system).

Suppose Dr. Warren had simply concluded that Michael is **emotionally disturbed**. That label would suggest a disturbance in the psychological system only, obscuring the fact that the biological, psychological, and social systems all require intervention.

It should be noted that categorizing can be helpful in grouping children for educational placement. A third-grade boy who is legally blind and is placed in a class for the **visually impaired** is probably more like the other children in that class in terms of educational needs than he is like children in a class for the **emotionally disturbed** or those in a regular third-grade class. It is important to keep in mind that while children in a class for the **visually impaired** are alike in some, or even many, ways, they are not **identical**.

A major problem with labels is that they can set off in the minds of parents, teachers, and a child's peers a complex chain of mental events referred to as a **self-fulfilling prophecy**

SELF – FULFILLING PROPHECY

W. I. Thomas, a sociologist, set forth a theorem basic to the social sciences: "If men define situations as real, they are real in their consequences" (Merton, 1948, p. 195). Merton explains this to mean that at times people respond primarily to the meaning a situation has for them, rather than to the objective features of the situation.

A **self-fulfilling prophecy** is, in the beginning, a false definition of a situation which, in turn, evokes new behaviors, making what was originally a false conception come true. For example, a classroom teacher may hold a stereotype in her mind of what a **learning disabled** child is like, even though she has not had actual experience with one. When her principal places a learning disabled boy in her second-grade class, the teacher may expect the boy to be hyperactive, immature, and doing work below grade level. Stereotyping operates at an unconscious level, meaning that the teacher is unaware that she holds such expectations.

The same teacher may fail to note academic progress made by the boy with a learning disability. Let's say the second grader's auditory learning disability was diagnosed early in first grade, and he has spent nearly a year with a speech-language pathologist improving his auditory skills and learning to read with phonics. When he enters second grade, he is reading at grade level. Despite this fact, his teacher puts him in the "yellow birds," her slowest reading group, because she is convinced that learning disabled children do not do grade-level work.

There is yet another aspect to a self-fulfilling prophecy, and that is that a teacher's expectations can actually influence a child's behavior in the direction of her prophecy. Prophecies can be either positive or negative and so can have positive or negative consequences for children's behavior.

A study by Rosenthal and Jacobson (1966, 1967, 1968a, 1968b) reveals the dynamics of a self-fulfilling prophecy in the classroom. The researchers went into an elementary school and told the staff that they would be administering the "Harvard Test of Inflected Acquisition" (an impressive-sounding test that did not exist) to all children in the school. In fact, what the researchers did was give intelligence tests to all the children and then pick twenty percent of the students in each grade at random, arbitrarily tagging them as "intellectual bloomers." Next, their classroom teachers were told that the "bloomers" would show unusual intellectual gains in the academic year ahead. The difference, then, between the children earmarked for intellectual growth and the undesignated control group existed only in the minds of the teachers.

At the end of the school year, all teachers were asked to rate each of the children on: 1) the extent to which they would be successful in the future, and 2) the degree to which they could be described as interesting, curious, happy, appealing, adjusted, affectionate, hostile, and motivated by a need for social approval.

As it turned out, teachers described the "bloomers" as having a significantly better chance of becoming successful in the future and as significantly more interesting, curious, and happy. There was a tendency, too, for these children to be seen as more appealing, adjusted, and affectionate, and as lower in the need for social approval. The children were again tested for intellectual functioning at the end of the year, and the "bloomers," the experimental group, gained more I.Q. points than the control group, although the control group members had also improved.

An interesting sidelight was the trend for the control group members, the "nonbloomers," to be regarded less favorably the more they gained intellectually. That finding suggests, according to the authors, that there may be "hazards to unexpected intellectual growth. Classroom teachers may not be prepared to assimilate the unexpected classroom behavior of the intellectually upwardly mobile child" (Rosenthal and Jacobson, 1967, p. 248).

Rosenthal (1973) proposes a four-factor theory to explain the link between teacher expectations and a child's behavior. He suggests that teachers who hold high expectations for certain students supply them with: 1) a warm socio-emotional climate (our systems term would be "environment"); 2) more material to be learned (inputs of information); 3) more opportunities to respond and question (outputs); and 4) more praise of correct performance (positive feedback), coupled with more corrections of wrong responses (negative feedback). Conversely, teachers who hold negative expectations for certain students provide them with a cool, impersonal climate, less material to master, few opportunities to respond, and little feedback, either positive or negative.

A strong asymmetry exists in teacher-pupil relationships, and teachers loom large in a child's mind as an important person to please. It is quite common for teachers to unconsciously hold **racial** and **social class stereotypes**. Still other stereotypes relate to **mental** and **physical handicaps**. A teacher may have negative expectations for a child because he or she is black (**racial** stereotype), poor (**social class** stereotype), retarded (**mental** stereotype), or blind (**physical** stereotype). A teacher's expectations function as inputs to the child-system and serve to alter a child's behavior in the direction of the prophecy.

In addition to negative expectations in regard to their learning ability, handicapped children must deal with an uneasiness felt by teachers, classmates, and even their parents when in the presence of someone who has a handicap. Jones (1977) explains that "people appear to be ill at ease around the mentally and physically handicapped and there is some indication that they attempt to cover their dis-ease with a patronizing kindness that is not really felt" (p. 114). This operates at an unconscious level, so that individuals are unaware of their own feelings and consequent actions toward the handicapped. While hidden from the ones experiencing them, these attitudes are usually all too clear to those on the receiving end.

When significant persons in the life of a handicapped child hold a bundle of expectations relating to the child's condition, it is probable that the child will live **down** to the expectations. Remember, a self-fulfilling prophecy is a **false** definition of a situation—in this case, a negative expectation for a child, based on a diagnostic label—which in turn produces a change in the child's behavior, making the originally false conception come true.

When we find, through diagnostic testing, that, let's say, a six-year-old girl is retarded, there are certain things we do know. For example, we know that a **retarded** child has limited intellectual functioning, delayed language, and will be slower than the normal child in learning academics. The label fails to tell us anything about her personality, motivation to learn, learning style, social skills, and special abilities, or about family and community support available to help counteract the disturbance. Labels do serve to show the severity of a problem. Terms such as **deaf/blind, multiply-handicapped**, and **cerebral palsied** spell out the need for intense, highly specialized services.

* * * * * *

In Chapter 3, we will take up biological essentials for learning. For the purpose of the study, we will be looking at the biological, psychological, and social systems separately, but we must remember that, in reality, these three systems are interdependent and intertwined and are impossible to separate.

Chapter 3

BIOLOGICAL ESSENTIALS FOR LEARNING

By the time Susan Carter's doctor confirms her suspicions that she is pregnant, her baby, Lyle, is already well along on the first and perhaps most important journey of his life—the one which begins at conception and ends at birth. Below Susan's level of conscious awareness, the baby-to-be is unfolding in a series of incredible stages of growth.

At conception, the union of the egg and sperm, the **genetic template** is laid down. Characteristics are freely and equally borrowed from Susan and her husband, producing a child who will be like, and yet unlike, his parents. Lyle will probably be very much like them in height, intellectual abilities, and coloring of skin, eyes, and hair; yet may be very different from them in temperament and talents.

GENETIC FACTORS

The basic units of heredity are **genes**. They are contained in 23 pairs of **chromosomes** present in every cell of the body. Genes are beads of information organized into strings which can only be seen with the aid of a microscope. In fact, the size of chromosomes borders on incomprehensible. Elam (1980) explains: "If a chromosome were removed from one of your cells, unfolded and laid out straight, it would have a length of about a yard, but it would be totally invisible. Ten thousand of them lying side by side would fit on the cut edge of a sheet of paper" (p. 30).

A single body contains 10,000 to 50,000 genes composed primarily of DNA molecules. Patlee (1981) explains that the DNA is "read by the cell in just as literal a sense as a computer reads a program" (p. 119).

In all the cells of the body except the sex cells, the microscopic bead-strings occur in pairs. In the sex cells, the pairs are split apart. In a process called **meiosis**, the members of each chromosomal pair split and move to opposite ends of the cell. The cell then splits into two cells, each of which contains 23 single chromosomes. This process occurs in both male and female parent cells to produce ovum and sperm. Each contains exactly one-half of the code necessary to program the development of a new human being. At conception, ovum and sperm come together, two halves making a whole to form a single cell having 23 pairs of chromosomes.

In a similar way, male and female chromosomes are formed. The male (xy) splits into an x and a y, and the female (xx) splits into an x and an x. These then combine to randomly produce xx and xy children, with the male parent (who has the y chromosome at his disposal) determining the sex of the offspring.

As we shall see in Chapter 4, the joining of genetic information of two parents is not always error-free. However, as we follow Lyle's development from a thought in his Dad's mind, "Wouldn't it be great to have a Lyle, Jr.?" to "It's a boy!" We will give him the benefit of all stages of development unfolding normally.

Multiple genes contribute to the development of almost all characteristics. Brain development, for example, is controlled by the interaction of at least 150 genes and probably more as yet unidentified. These, in turn, interact with environmental variants to produce the behavioral reflection of this characteristic in the individual child. As Gould (1981) explains, genes do not make "specific bits and pieces of a body; they code for a range of forms under an array of environmental conditions." Of importance in educating children is the fact that even when a trait has been "built and set, environmental intervention may still modify inherited defects" (p. 156).

Chromosomes settle themselves into an "X" pattern within the cell. This "X" configuration results from two chromosomes joining at their midpoints and bending away from each other. Not just any two chromosomes join together, only those which are both concerned with specific traits, like color of hair or eyes. The related gene pairs for a given trait are called alleles. Alleles are said to be homozygous when cells have matching genes for a specific characteristic. In contrast, they are heterozygous when cells have different genes for the same trait.

A **dominant gene** is one whose trait appears in the individual even when that gene is paired with a different gene for the trait. It overpowers a **recessive gene,** which must be paired with another recessive one in order to express.

For the sake of simplicity, let's imagine that hair color is a single gene pair trait. Let's let capital "B" represent the genetic code for brown hair, which is dominant. Lower case "b" stands for the code for blonde, which is recessive. Of the combinations which may occur, **BB, Bb,** and **bB** will produce brown hair; only **bb** will result in blonde hair.

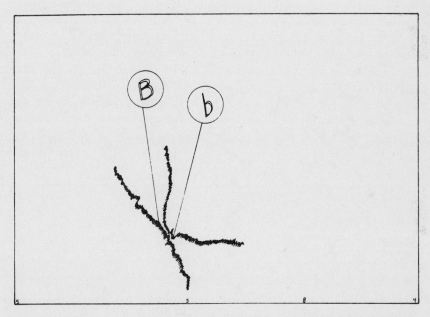

Figure 3-1. Genes are arranged on chromosomes in bead-like strings. Lyle's genotype for hair color is Bb. A gene for brown hair (B) came from his mother, a gene for blond hair (b) from his father.

As Figure 3-1 shows, Susan has brown hair (BB) and Lyle, Sr., has blonde hair (bb). Each parent then has only one gene possibility to offer to the pairing. Their baby can only have a Bb combination which will express as brown hair. However, a perfect relationship does not exist between **genotype** (the nature of the information about a trait as it is coded in the genes) and **phenotype** (the way the trait will appear in Lyle).

As McCall (1975) explains, dominance does not have to be all or none; in fact, gradations are more likely. For Lyle, this would translate to shades of hair color from pure brunette through mousey brown to dishwater blonde. At the point of Lyle's conception, we are privileged to genotype information only (Bb). We will have to wait until Lyle is several months old and has sufficient hair to describe his phenotype.

LIFE IN THE WOMB

At the point of conception, Lyle has only just begun; nine more months of development within his mother's body await him. The first two weeks after conception is called the **germinal period**. The task of this period is primarily cell division, as the fertilized egg anchors itself to the lining of Susan's uterus. The next six weeks are referred to as the **embryonic period**; organ systems are now beginning to form. By the end of this period, the organism is almost an inch long and appears human. From about eight weeks past conception to birth, it is known as a **fetus**.

The mother is the sole source of nourishment for an unborn child. Even before her pregnancy is confirmed, Susan begins reading books on nutrition. She notes that the sources vary with respect to the required amounts of vitamins and minerals and whether or not supplements are considered necessary. To find out what would be best for her personally, she consults a **nutritionist** who studies Susan's typical daily food intake and outlines a plan for providing optimal nutrition for two.

To begin with, Susan's **protein** intake is increased by two-thirds, i.e., from 44 to 74 grams per day. Protein is responsible for building a baby's hard and soft body tissues, forming its brain, and making the placenta. Susan's intake of the minerals, **calcium**, **phosphorus**, and **magnesium**, which are needed to build a baby's bones, is increased by 50 percent. Because few women start pregnancy with sufficient **iron** stored in their bodies, due to the regular loss during menstruation, iron supplements of 60 milligrams a day are recommended.

As for vitamins, Susan's **folic acid** requirements will double. A B-vitamin, its role is to help build the developing immune system. Another B-vitamin, B_6 is critical to support the unfolding of a baby's central nervous system. Susan is given a 50 milligram supplement of B_6. In addition, Susan's intake of vitamin A is increased by one-fourth, to promote healthy skin and linings of baby's internal organs; vitamin C by one-third, to enhance her body's use of **iron, folic acid**, and vitamin A; and vitamin D by 100 percent, to permit her to use **calcium** properly (Brody, 1981; Gerras, 1977; Padus, 1981).

Confident of giving her baby and herself the best of prenatal care, Susan carefully follows her nutritional plan and continues her work as a librarian. Her energy level is high; her health, good.

Meanwhile, Lyle is becoming accustomed to the noises and sensations within his mother's body. He hears frequent rumblings in Susan's stomach, voices belonging to both parents, and, most importantly, the steady rhythmic thump of the maternal heartbeat (Verny, 1981). Susan is typing card catalogue entries one rainy afternoon when Lyle signals his readiness to be born.

BIRTH

As the process of pregnancy comes to a close, labor begins. In the first stage of labor, Susan feels faint contractions which grow stronger and more frequent. Because she has elected to have a home delivery, her first call is to her midwife and then to Lyle who picks her up at work.

Both Susan and Lyle favored a home birth because Susan's general health is good, complications were not anticipated, and because Lyle wanted to take an active part in the birth process. At the initial meeting with the midwife, Susan's medical history was taken, and she was advised to receive traditional prenatal care from her family doctor or gynecologist, in addition to keeping regular contacts with her midwife.

Two weeks before her due date, Susan and Lyle began preparing their bedroom for use as a delivery room. They were instructed to carefully clean the room, wipe down all furniture with a disinfectant, and sterilize sheets, towels, baby clothes, and the clothes Susan would wear immediately following delivery.

Once at home, Susan makes a few calls, moves around as long as it feels comfortable to do so, and has a light meal. The midwife makes periodic checks of Susan's blood pressure and temperature and the baby's heartbeat.

The second stage of labor begins once the cervix, the opening to the uterus, is completely dilated. After the midwife checks to make sure the baby is positioned head down, delivery begins. Employing Leboyer's methods (Leboyer, 1976), the lights are dimmed in the delivery area and voices are hushed. Besides Lyle, Sr., Susan's mother is present for the delivery.

As he moves down the birth canal, the contractions of Susan's uterus stimulate her baby's skin. According to Montagu (1978), uterine contractions serve much the same function as does the licking of offspring by animals; both serve to activate the newborn's brain and central nervous system for functioning outside the mother's body. As soon as the baby boy is removed, whimpering a bit, but not crying, he is placed on his mother's stomach. The midwife now takes the first Apgar reading, repeating it in five minutes. This is a routine procedure for evaluating a baby's pulse, breathing, muscle tone, reflex irritability, and color (from blue to pink). Lyle is a nine on the ten-point scale. It is noteworthy that Lyle would have scored ten points if he had cried at birth; however, babies delivered by Leboyer methods usually do not cry.

Montagu stresses that for human offspring, gestation is not complete when a baby is born. Why, then, must babies enter the world before they are fully ready to survive its rigors? "The explanation seems to be that the fetus must be born when its head has reached the maximum size compatible with its passage through the birth canal. This transmigration constitutes no mean accomplishment. Indeed, the passage through the four inches of the birth canal is the most hazardous journey a human being ever takes" (Montagu, 1978, p. 43).

The Apgar is the first formal assessment of the integrity of a child's **biological system**. Recall that this system is contained within the boundary of the skin. **Psychological** and **social systems** of a child, just as real and as important as the biological system, are more

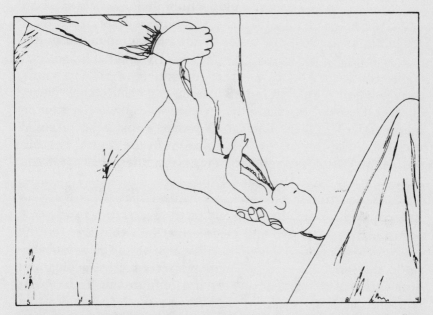

Figure 3-2. The biological system is bounded by the skin. The Apgar is the first formal assessment of a child's biological system.

difficult to describe because no tangible boundary surrounds them. While birth is not the **end** of gestation, it is a transition from one phase of development to another. "With birth the newborn moves into a wholly new zone of experience and adaptation, from an aquatic solitary existence into an atmospheric and social environment" (Montagu, 1978, p. 60). There will be more about a baby's early social relationships in later chapters.

After removal of the placenta, the umbilical cord is cut. The baby is now placed in a tub of warm water, two degrees above body temperature, and he is bathed by his father. After Susan showers and puts on fresh clothes, she returns to breastfeed her baby.

INFANCY AND CHILDHOOD

The process of growth and development begun in the womb continues throughout **infancy**, the first two years of life, and childhood. Genetic limits and ranges were set at conception, and the child now proceeds to develop within them. The most easily observed stages of development are referred to as **motor** and **language milestones,** and they are triggered by the maturation of the brain.

Since Susan is breastfeeding Lyle, he is being provided with all the nutrients needed for the first six months of life. Mother's milk contains **exactly** what a baby needs in terms of protein, carbohydrates, fat, and minerals. Its vitamin content depends upon the vitamin intake of the mother. The fat in human milk is an essential nutrient important for the development of the central nervous system. Milk also has immunological properties which protect a baby from infection (Brostrøm, 1981).

Lyle's first night convinces his parents that he is truly an individual. Expecting to be up and down several times to comfort him, they are surprised and pleased that he sleeps through the night. Lyle's sleep cycles are much like Susan's and were probably set in the womb. In addition, he is very regular in feeding and elimination cycles and seems, even at one month, to be even-tempered and easy to get along with. Research has shown that there is an inborn aspect of temperament.

Temperament

In an attempt to identify inborn patterns of temperament, Alexander Thomas and his co-workers, Stella Chess and Herbert Birch, began a longitudinal study to follow the interaction of temperament and environment in specific children, beginning in the first few months of life (Thomas, 1976). Their search was for **genetic** and **constitutional factors** which might influence later psychological development. They defined nine categories of temperament:

- **Activity Level.** The motor component of a child's functioning observed in bathing, eating, playing, dressing, reaching, crawling, and walking.
- **Rhythmicity.** The regularity of sleep-wake cycles, feeding, and elimination.
- **Approach/Withdrawal.** A baby's response to a new stimulus such as a new toy or a new food.
- **Adaptability.** The ease with which a child adapts to new situations.

- **Threshold of Responsiveness.** The intensity of a sensation, object, or person necessary to evoke a measurable response from a child.
- **Intensity of Reaction.** The energy level of a response.
- **Quality of Mood.** The amount of pleasant, joyful, and friendly behavior as opposed to unpleasant, crying, and unfriendly behavior.
- **Distractibility.** The effectiveness of outside stimuli in breaking up ongoing behavior.
- **Attention Span and Persistence.** The first term refers to the length of time an activity is pursued by the child, and the second, to the continuation of an activity in the presence of outside competing stimuli.

The researchers found that the characteristics of infants studied tended to fall into temperament constellations. One such cluster included: Regularity, positive approach responses to new stimuli, high adaptability to changes, and a preponderantly positive mood of mild to moderate intensity. Children with this cluster of characteristics the researchers referred to as **easy** children. These are the children who can be easily handled even by first-time parents or parents under stress.

Another cluster included: Irregularity in biological functions, mostly withdrawal responses to new stimuli, no or slow adabtability to change, frequent negative mood, and predominantly intense reactions. These children, who try the patience of a saint, they called **difficult** children. Experienced, relaxed parents would probably find these children difficult to handle, and they are especially trying for first-time parents.

A third cluster combined: Negative responses of mild intensity to new stimuli with slow adaptability after repeated contact. These children were referred to as **slow to warm up.**

These and other studies point to a **biological system** component in temperament which later plays a part in the development of **personality,** or the **psychological system.** Children are individuals from the moment they enter the world. Mother-child and family-child interactions can modify inborn temperament characteristics but cannot supplant them.

Lyle's cluster of temperament behaviors would qualify him as being an **easy child**. Susan notes that his development continues to unfold rhythmically and easily.

Language and Motor Milestones

Lyle will pass through a number of predictable stages as he acquires motor and language skills. Typically, children alternate between the two areas of development, directing their energies first toward one and then the other.

For the most part, the normal unfolding of stages is dependent upon the integrity of the **biological system**, particularly the brain. In turn, the status of the brain is dependent upon guidelines in the genetic template, freedom from injury at birth, and inputs to it in the form of food and information. Adequately nourishing the brain is particularly important during the first two years of an infant's life. Susan began her pregnancy nutrition-conscious, and now she is careful to see that Lyle has a balanced diet. To insure this, she makes her own baby food from fresh fruits and vegetables and leftover meat she has cooked.

Adequate information in the form of stimulation is also critical to the developing brain. In this chapter, however, we will focus primarily on the biological essentials of development, filling in the psychological and social components in Chapters 6 and 9, respectively.

Lyle is a born communicator. In the first few days of his life, he is responsive to sound and moves his head toward its source. His biological drive to speak is as strong and as basic as are his other drives—to eat, sleep, eliminate, and be held. The premise that the ability to communicate is inborn is supported by the observation that all healthy children around the globe acquire their language at about the same speed "independently of whether they are deprived children or children brought up by doting parents who drill them in language skills" (Farb, 1974, p. 10).

The first sounds Lyle makes, at about three months, are vowel-like, gurgling sounds called **cooing**. His motor task during this period is to support his head while lying on his stomach. By the time Lyle sits up, at five months, his cooing is sprinkled with consonant sounds and now qualifies as **babbling**. In his sound play,

Lyle strings together sounds in much the same way he will later string beads on a shoelace, the patterns accidental at first, and later, intentional. At this stage, "mama" and "dada" are probably accidental, although Lyle is clearly pleased by the response they bring from the adults in his life. By his seventh month, the combinations of sound and stress patterns resemble adult speech. Lyle plainly has something to say, although he is not yet able to say it plainly.

In his eighth month, Lyle begins to crawl, getting up onto his hands and knees and moving forward—right arm and left leg moving together and left arm and right leg together. Susan does not confine Lyle to a walker or a playpen, encouraging him instead to crawl free as long as he likes.

At nine months, Lyle gives his first indication that he is beginning to understand some single words. While dressing him one day, Susan says, "Help mama; hand me your shoe,"—Surprise! —Lyle reaches for it, and mother and baby are thrilled.

As babbling winds down, single words break through. The lips are of importance during the first year, primarily because of their function in nursing. A child's first words usually appear at about the end of the first year and begin with sounds made with the lips (p, b, and m) and tongue (t, d, and n). It should come as no surprise then that the earliest words a baby speaks are "mama," papa," "dada," and "nana." The words for mother and father, the world around, begin with lip and tongue sounds, almost as if it were by design that baby should find them easy to say (Farb, 1974).

Lyle's first word, at 11 months, is "mama," quickly followed by "dada," "bye," "hi," and "up." From age one to two, new words are added at a rapid fire rate. Lyle now has words for favorite toys, animals, clothing, and household items. Some words appear to be entirely of Lyle's own making, such as "too-ree" for scissors or "shoo-shing" for his cousin, Lauren. Other words come out sounding the way they do to Lyle's not-yet-mature perceptual system. Thus, "tat" for "cat," "pish" for "fish," and "doydan" for "Aunt Joy Ann."

When speaking, Lyle intends more than he can say. For example, "shoe" may mean, "I want my shoe on," "I want my shoe off," or, perhaps, "I can't find my shoe." With context cues and a great deal of patience on Susan's part, the meaning usually becomes clear.

By two, Lyle's single word vocabulary is about fifty words. It seems that Lyle has no sooner blown out the candles on his second birthday cake when the two-word stage emerges. Whereas only a few months before, "baby" sufficed, now Lyle says "my baby," meaning "mama, come find my baby doll." Lyle is not just repeating what has been said to him, as one might suspect. In fact, even his earliest sentences are of his own creation. Because of an innate capacity to do so, Lyle is acquiring a grammar that can generate an infinite number of new sentences. Until this point, Lyle's vocabulary has consisted of some nouns, some action words, and some modifiers. Now he combines them to make sentences he has never heard before. "Baby truck," "truck blue," and "baby blue!" (after sticking his hand in a bucket of blue paint) are of his own making. Lyle is more vocal now in expressing his desires. "More meat, more meat, more meat," he chants at the dinner table to his parents who, engaged in conversation, do not notice that he has finished his serving of pork chop.

As for motor skills, by two Lyle ambulates with ease and can climb up stairs unassisted. He can now make getaways from his parents quite easily, and they learn to watch him more carefully than before in shopping malls and at the grocery store.

Lyle's grandparents give him a tricycle for his third birthday, and he gleefully jumps on his present, riding it for the first time with ease. Following this birthday, the process of adding new vocabulary words slows a bit, and Lyle's sentence length begin to expand. He now talks in sentences of three or more words. His sentences contain articles ("I see the ball"), plurals ("more peas"), prepositions ("ball on table"), and past tense ("I goed to the ball game"), although all forms may not be used correctly. At three, Lyle's speech still contains a few sound substitutions, but these are dropping out.

By the time Lyle turns four, rapid advances in language and motor abilities heighten his awareness of self and his self-confidence. At a playground, Lyle swings by himself, goes down the slide unassisted, and climbs on the jungle gym, often stopping to remind his father, "Watch me!" Back at home, Lyle delights in relating his adventures of the morning to his mother. His speech is now almost a hundred percent intelligible. Only one sound substitution remains, w/r, which is most noticeable when Lyle talks about the "Eastuh wabbit."

By five, Lyle is throwing a ball, turning somersaults, and taking swimming lessons at the "Y." Lyle now has a grasp of the passage of time. Weekend days are recognized as Saturday and Sunday, rather than "cartoon day" and "church day." Lyle asks many **wh-** questions, "**When** is the circus coming?" "**Why** can't I have a pony?" "**Where** do babies come from?" and "**What** does 'brat' mean?" For the most part, Lyle sounds like an adult when he speaks. There are times when Lyle may still express himself with words or word combinations of his own making. When his preschool teacher shows the class a picture of a cactus and asks who can tell the name of it, Lyle waves his hand, confidently calling it an "ouch cowboy!"

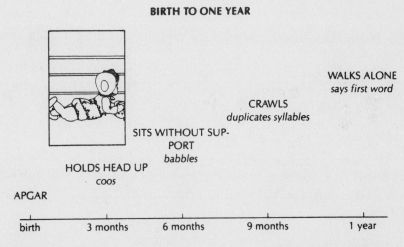

Figure 3-3. Biological system milestones in *language* and MOTOR development (birth to one year).

Figures 3-3 and 3-4 summarize the language and accompanying motor milestones of the first five years of a child's life. For a more detailed listing of language milestones, see the **Verbal Language Development Scale** (Mecham, 1971), and of motor milestones, see

18 MONTHS TO FIVE YEARS

TURNS SOMERSAULT
talks almost like an adult

GOES DOWN SLIDE WITH-
OUT HELP
recites a nursery rhyme

PEDALS TRICYCLE
*makes sentences of 3 or
more words*

RUNS
combines two words

CLIMBS STAIRS
adds many new words

| 18 months | 2 years | 3 years | 4 years | 5 years |

Figure 3-4. Biological system milestones in *language* and MOTOR development
(18 months to 5 years).

the **Denner Developmental Screening Test** (Frankenburg, Dodds, and
Fandal, 1970).

When reading charts, it is important to keep in mind that they
are based on the **average** age certain milestones are reached.
"Normal" is highly variable. While Lyle said his first word at 11
months, another child may not speak until 17 months and still
develop normal language skills.

Guidelines for assessment of the **biological system** will be found
in Chapter 5. For now, it is sufficient to say that we do not look for
isolated events which are behind schedule, but, rather, for **patterns**
of delay.

* * * * * *

In this chapter, we have explored the normal development of a
child's biological system. We have followed Lyle from conception
through his fifth year, and everything has gone right. In Chapter
4, we will look at possible disturbances at each of the critical stages
of development and at learning disorders which can result.

Chapter 4

DISTRESS IN THE BIOLOGICAL SYSTEM

While our imaginary child from Chapter 3, Lyle, had every advantage in his unfolding from a single cell to a baby, tens of thousands of children born each year are not so fortunate. Distress can occur in the biological system at each of its major turning points—conception, in the womb, and at birth—and as development continues its steady course into infancy and childhood.

Some handicapping conditions can be traced to one specific point of distress; others can be produced at all major developmental points; still others are of unknown etiology. The handicapping conditions of concern to us are those which adversely affect a child's **brain** and/or **input channels** of seeing, hearing, and touch. Such disturbances serve to disrupt the normal learning process.

Our perspective in this chapter will be from **aboard** the cause and effect train, meaning that we will be viewing system distress and resulting handicaps as they come about. This is a very different perspective from that of a professional taking a history years after the fact.

The name of a child's handicapping condition does not necessarily reveal what his or her special education placement will be. Many terms for handicapping conditions refer to physical anomalies, such as **cleft palate, cerebral palsy,** or **hydrocephalus.** Such terms give no clue as to special education placement. For example, one child with cleft palate may have normal intelligence, be mainstreamed for all classwork, and go to speech therapy once a week; another child with cleft palate may be learning disabled and need a self-contained lab; a third cleft palate child may need a class for the educably retarded. Only psychological and educational evaluation could determine the proper educational program and placement for these three children.

In this chapter, we will discover possible points of distress to the

Table 4-I

EDUCATIONAL LABELS OF CHILDREN WHOSE PRIMARY DISTRESS
IS TO THE BIOLOGICAL SYSTEM

Mentally Retarded
Hearing Impaired
Visually Impaired
Speech and Language Disordered
Learning Disabled
Physically Handicapped

developing biological system. Table 4-I contains a list of educational labels which tend to follow **primary** disturbance to the biological system. This means that a child's disturbance **originated** within the biological system, even though its effects may have spread to other systems.

Also in this chapter, we will meet four children who represent each of the four possible points of biological distress: (1) **genetic distress,** (2) **distress in the womb,** (3) **distress at birth,** and (4) **distress in infancy and childhood.** These children will be followed into Chapter 5, where a treatment program for each is presented.

GENETIC DISTRESS

At conception, the merging of genetic information from egg and sperm, a number of handicapping conditions can result. Within the nucleus of every cell of the body are 22 pairs of chromosomes—the **autosomes,** plus the sex chromosomes, xx and xy. Inheritance of a handicap may be either **autosomal** or **sex-linked.** Recessive genes are the culprits in most hereditary defects, and one must appear in combination with another in order to express. Elam (1980) explains that as a rule defects of physiology and of enzyme systems are transmitted by recessive genes, and defects of body structure, such as cleft palate or club foot, by dominant genes.

Chromosomes are numbered from the largest pair, number one, to the smallest, number 22. Defects are most often associated with nine of the chromosome pairs; specifically, numbers 4, 5, 13, 14, 15, 17, 18, 21, and 22 (Rugh and Shettles, 1971). One chromosome of a pair may be missing, an extra chromosome may be present, or an abnormal chromosome may occur which has either too much or too little genetic material (Krishef, 1983).

Genetic distress is a factor in many handicapping conditions, including Down Syndrome, mental retardation, inborn errors of metabolism, hearing and vision impairment, speech and language disorders, learning disabilities, cerebral palsy, cleft palate, and hydrocephalus.

Down Syndrome

The appearance of three chromosomes in place of the usual two is called trisomy. An extra chromosome present in pair number 21 produces Down Syndrome or trisomy 21. While Down children tend to have a distinctive appearance at birth, only a chromosome test can confirm or rule out a doctor's suspicion.

In childhood, Down Syndrome children tend to be short and stocky. Their hands are short and broad, and their fingers, stubby. A single crease, termed a simian crease, runs across their palms. Another characteristic of Down children is the presence of epicanthal folds, tiny folds of skin, at the inside corner of the eyes.

In terms of intelligence, Down children usually fall into either the educable or trainable range of retardation. An educable child's intelligence, as measured by standardized intelligence testing such as the Wechsler Scales, falls in the 50 to 75 range. The average range of intelligence is 90 to 110. Educable refers to a child's ability to be educated, to learn to read, spell, and do arithmetic. In their early years, these children usually are mildly delayed in language and motor milestones. In the school years, educable children are taught academics. The eventual level reached in this area depends upon individual abilities. Most educable children have the potential, with training, to do some type of routine work as adults and to live independently. Children whose intelligence is in the trainable range score between 25 and 50 on intelligence testing. Their delays in language and motor milestones are more marked than those of the educable child, and so they may be diagnosed earlier, beginning specialized classes in the preschool years. Children whose intellectual functioning is in the trainable range usually do not learn academic skills. Educational programs for them stress self-help and social skills. With supervision, some are able to work in sheltered workshops in their teen and adult years.

Mental Retardation

As we learned in Chapter 3, at least 150 genes are known to contribute to the development of the brain. Inheritance accounts for the retardation of many children, even though it may be so distant as to be untraceable. Very often children born with inherited patterns of retardation have a normal physical appearance at birth, and their problems do not become evident until infancy or the preschool years.

Inborn Errors of Metabolism

A child born with a metabolic disorder is unable to make adequate use of certain chemicals needed for growth. Metabolic disorders are progressive, and result in mental retardation. For most, there is no known cure. One such disorder which can be successfully treated is Phenylketonuria (PKU), abnormal protein metabolism. PKU can be identified with blood and urine tests immediately following birth. By placing a child with PKU on a special diet, retardation can be prevented.

Hearing Impairment

Of the two basic types of hearing impairment, **deafness** is a complete loss of functional hearing; the other, **hearing loss,** is a loss of a percentage of hearing which can usually be improved with the use of a hearing aid. **Sensori-neural** losses can be produced by genetic defects either in the inner ear or in the auditory nerve which transmits electrical impulses to the brain. **Conductive** losses are caused by an interference in the middle ear, such as fluid which blocks the transmission of sound from the outer to the inner ear.

Vision Impairment

To be termed **educationally blind**, one must have a loss of sight so severe that braille is required to learn to read. The loss of a **percentage of sight** may require special glasses or the use of large print. Inherited conditions which may affect the eye are glaucoma (abnormal development of the mechanism which drains fluid in the eye), cataracts (an opaque lens which interferes with vision), and diseases of the retina.

Speech and Language Disorders

Children may have speech and language disorders even though they are not hearing impaired or retarded. As a group, these disorders include delays in understanding language, verbal expression, and articulation. Speech and language problems tend to run in families, indicating a hereditary component.

Children with **autism** and **childhood schizophrenia** display unique patterns of disturbance in the areas of verbal and nonverbal communication. Biological distress may well play a part in autism and childhood schizophrenia; however, both disorders have traditionally been considered as disturbances of the psychological system, and so will be discussed in detail in Chapter 7.

Learning Disabilities

Children with learning disabilities have difficulty with reading, spelling, and math, despite normal intelligence and normal sensory acuity. Learning disability in children is often accompanied by **attention deficit disorder** and **hyperactivity**. Those with attention deficit disorder are easily distracted, impulsive, and tend to act before thinking. Hyperactivity refers to excessive, uncontrollable motor movements. Learning disabilities are known to run in families.

Cerebral Palsy

Cerebral palsy is primarily a motor disability produced by a lesion in the motor control centers of the brain. Depending upon the extent of the lesion, the motor disability may occur in combination with language, speech, and intellectual impairments. Genetic factors appear to play a part in only a small percentage of children who have cerebral palsy.

Cleft Palate

Clefts may involve either the hard and soft regions of the palate, the upper lip, or may appear in combination. Clefts of the palate interfere with articulation and give a nasal quality to a child's speech. Inheritance accounts for a large percentage of cleft lip and palate in children.

Hydrocephalus

Hydrocephalus is the result of an abnormal accumulation of fluid in the cranium which produces an enlarged head. Retardation is inevitable unless the fluid can be shunted and pressure relieved. Heredity is implicated in only a small percentage of cases.

A number of genetic disorders can be prevented if future parents seek counseling with a geneticist before a child is conceived. The geneticist takes a family history and checks the genetic makeup of each prospective parent to discover genes responsible for inherited disabilities.

A second preventive measure available after conception has occurred is the identification of a genetic problem within the womb and termination of the pregnancy. The most relied upon procedure for this is amniocentesis. Performed between the fourteenth and sixteenth week after conception, a sample of amniotic fluid is withdrawn by inserting a hollow needle through the mother's abdomen. Fetal cells from the amniotic fluid are then grown in a culture to detect possible chromosomal abnormalities in the cells. Moore (1982) recommends amniocentesis when one of the following factors is present during a pregnancy: (1) late maternal age; (2) previous birth of a Down Syndrome child; (3) chromosomal abnormality in either parent; (4) women who are carriers of X-linked recessive disorders; (5) brain and spinal cord defects in the family, and (6) carriers of inborn errors of metabolism.

A less common procedure for identifying problems within the womb is **fetoscopy** which involves the use of lighted instruments to look at parts of the fetal body. The fetoscope is introduced through the abdominal wall and the uterine wall into the amniotic cavity, similar to the way the needle is inserted in amniocentesis. The fetus can be scanned for congenital malformations such as cleft palate. Another method, **ultrasonography**, produces an ultrasound scan of the fetus and can reveal a condition such as hydrocephalus.

GENETIC DISTRESS – MARIAN

Ruth Hammond was in her midthirties when she gave up her career as a concert pianist, married a college professor, and began teaching piano at a small college. Eager to start a family, Ruth and Guy had their first child, a daughter, a year later. A second daughter, born a year and a half after the first, died at birth of unknown causes. At age 40, Ruth is pregnant for the third time.

Marian is born after 22 hours of labor. Exhausted, Ruth falls asleep after hearing the baby is a girl. Hours later, when she awakens, Guy and her obstetrician are in her room talking in hushed voices. The distressed looks on their faces causes her to fear the worst, that this baby has also died. But, instead, the doctor says, "Ruth, your baby has Down Syndrome. In addition, she has respiratory problems, which we'll treat as best we can. Beyond that, there is no doubt that she'll be retarded. It might be best to plan for her institutional care before you leave the hospital."

DISTRESS IN THE WOMB

Handicapping conditions which occur within the womb are referred to as **congenital**. Because they have their origin at this stage of development, they cannot be passed on to future generations.

Each organ of the developing child has a critical period in its development, which is the time of most rapid cell division. It is during this period that the organ is most vulnerable to assault from what are called teratogens. Moore (1982) defines a teratogen as "any agent that can induce or increase the incidence of a congenital malformation" (p. 153).

All periods of development appear to be critical where the brain is concerned. The brain begins its development in the womb at about 18 days and approaches its adult size, weight, and number of cells by age two. Restak (1979) describes two overlapping stages of brain development. The first stage begins in the second trimester and continues into the second year of life. It is marked by rapid nerve cell multiplication. The second stage lasts from the third trimester until the baby is about six months of age. During this stage, the dendrites are formed which establish synapses, the means of communication between neurons.

Potential harm to the brain lurks within the shelter of the womb. Some factors which are associated with congenital malformations are maternal age, infections, nutritional deficits, drugs, radiation, multiple pregnancy, the Rh factor, and maternal stress.

Maternal Age

Women who are high-risk for giving birth to children with handicapping conditions are those older than 37 and younger than 17. A higher percentage of mentally retarded children are born to very young and very old mothers.

Infections

The most common infection which is known to produce birth defects is rubella, or German measles. While the mother may experience it as nothing more than a light rash, it can have devastating effects on the child she is carrying. If the mother is infected during the first trimester of her pregnancy, the baby may have multiple handicaps such as hearing impairment, vision impairment, mental retardation, and cerebral palsy. Cytomegalovirus, a herpes virus, can cause blindness, deafness, dental deformities, and mental retardation, when transmitted by a pregnant mother to her fetus in the first three months of fetal life.

Nutritional Deficits

Poor maternal diet can result in the development of fewer brain cells in the fetus she is carrying. Deficits in protein and specific vitamins and minerals may produce learning problems ranging from language and speech disorders to mental retardation, depending upon the extent of the deficit.

Drugs

Here we include the effects of prescription drugs and over-the-counter medications such as antacids, antihistamines, and aspirin. Because all drugs are capable of crossing the placenta from mother to child, all can be considered potentially dangerous. This list includes alcohol, nicotine, and possibly caffeine. Excessive alcohol intake during pregnancy is known to cause growth deficiency and mental retardation. Cigarette smoking retards physical growth of the fetus and brain development. Smoking also reduces the amount of oxygen available to the child. While caffeine is not yet a proven teratogen, studies of its effects are underway, and there is enough evidence to suggest that it should be avoided during pregnancy.

Radiation

There is no evidence that diagnostic x-ray can cause congenital malformations. However, therapeutic x-ray, such as that given to a woman with cancer of the cervix, is known to produce skeletal abnormalities, cleft palate, and mental retardation.

Multiple Pregnancy

Children born of a multiple pregnancy tend to weigh less, and low birth weight is associated with language and speech disorders and mental retardation.

Rh Factor

This refers to an incompatibility of blood between mother and fetus. When the mother's blood is Rh negative and the fetus's blood is Rh positive, the fetus produces antigens which are passed through the placenta into the mother's blood. Her blood in turn makes antibodies that are returned through the placenta to the blood of the fetus. The resulting problems for the baby include anemia and brain damage. Injury to the brain can result in mental retardation, speech and language disorders, cerebral palsy, or vision and hearing impairment.

Maternal Stress

It is now a widely accepted fact that psychologically-experienced stress can produce changes in an individual's physiology, producing physical illness. When the person under stress is a female and pregnant, the stress she is experiencing can in turn affect the biological development of the child she is carrying. Emotional stress during the first trimester of the pregnancy can result in ill health for the baby in the early months of its life, mental retardation, and physical malformation. Stress during the latter months of pregnancy may produce a baby who is irritable, hyperactive, and has feeding problems (Elam, 1980).

DISTRESS IN THE WOMB—OWEN

Louise Powell became pregnant with her second child less than a year after her first child, a boy, was born. She was still dieting to lose the weight from her first pregnancy when she discovered that she was pregnant again. Determined not to gain so much weight this time, she continued to cut back on her food intake. A hard winter in Chicago confined Louise to the house most of the day with her baby. She found herself fretful and tense, looking forward more and more to an afterfive drink with her husband, Steve. When his work kept him late at the office, she drank alone.

At two weeks past her due date, labor was induced, and Louise delivered a six-pound boy. Despite the sedation, she was aware that she did not hear the baby cry. The following day, her doctor told her that Owen was unable to breathe on his own at birth and had to be given oxygen.

DISTRESS AT BIRTH

In a normal birth, the baby moves down the birth canal which is composed of the bony pelvis and the soft tissues of the cervix and vagina, and, then, appears, head first. The cervix increases from a diameter of less than a centimeter to approximately ten centimeters to permit the baby to move from its mother's body into the doctor's or midwife's waiting arms.

The uterine contractions are involuntary. They begin as far apart as 20 to 30 minutes and become closer together and more intense until their recurrence is as often as two to three minutes apart. These involuntary contractions, coupled with the mother's conscious efforts to push, expel the baby.

The normal first sound a baby makes is either a fullbodied cry or a whimper. Hoarse, high-pitched, whining, or feeble cries usually are indicative of problems internal to the baby (Illingworth, 1980).

The main concern for the child during birth is that it receive sufficient oxygen. Either loss of oxygen, **anoxia,** or an injury to the fetal head can permanently damage a baby's central nervous system, producing a number of handicaps, including cerebral palsy, vision and hearing impairments, retardation, and speech and language disorders. Incidents at birth associated with later learning problems are described in Jensen, Benson, and Bobak (1977). These include **breech birth, prematurity, a small-for-dates baby, problems with the umbilical cord, hemorrhaging by the mother, forceps delivery, drugs administered during labor, and Caesarean.**

Breech Birth

When a baby's buttocks or feet are near the cervical opening and come out first, this is referred to as breech presentation. Breech birth occurs in about three percent of all deliveries. Because the fetal head is last to deliver, it is critical for the mother's pelvis to be sufficiently large to allow it to pass un-damaged.

Prematurity

An infant born before completing the 37th or 38th week of gestation, irrespective of birth weight, is referred to as premature. Because the blood vessels of premature babies are more perme-able and fragile than those of full-term babies, sudden change in pressure at birth can lead to the breaking of a vessel, resulting in cerebral hemorrhage and brain damage. Premature babies are also more susceptible to respiratory distress syndrome (RDS), because they are not yet fully prepared to breathe on their own.

Small-For-Dates

Babies who are small-for-dates evidence inadequate growth for their gestational age. Maternal smoking and nutritional deficits can be responsible.

Problems with the Umbilical Cord

The umbilical cord may be cut before the infant is breathing on its own, thus eliminating its oxygen supply. The cord may also become twisted during birth, interrupting the flow of blood and oxygen from mother to baby.

Hemorrhaging by the Mother

When a woman hemorrhages during delivery, the flow of blood to baby is diminished, reducing its oxygen supply.

Forceps Delivery

In a forceps delivery, two spoonlike blades are used to extract the fetal head. These instruments are used when it is necessary to shorten the second stage of difficult labor or when the mother is too fatigued to push the child out, or when a fetus is in danger and must be delivered quickly. Injuries to the newborn most often result from what is termed a **high forceps** delivery. In such a delivery, the baby's head has descended and is entering the pelvis but is not yet engaged. The doctor, reaching into the birth canal to extract the child, cannot see where the forceps are being placed. As a result, there is danger to the baby of skull fracture and cerebral hemorrhage.

Drugs during Labor

General anesthetics and drugs given to a woman to promote rapid labor can reduce the oxygen content of the mother's blood and, therefore, limit the oxygen available to the fetus.

Caesarean

Situations which indicate a Caesarean birth, or a "C-Section," include an infant too large to pass through the mother's pelvis, a scar in the uterus left by a previous Caesarean, hemorrhage or the threat of it, and fetal distress.

Caesarean is a major operation performed under anesthesia. It involves removing the infant from the uterus by way of an incision in the abdominal wall and the uterus. Children born by Caesarean do not have the wrinkles and bruises typical of those who have squeezed down the birth canal. However, they do not receive the stimulation to the central nervous system provided by uterine contractions and so are more susceptible to all types of learning problems.

Many hospitals have clinics set up to treat children who experience distress at birth. A **neonatologist** is a medical doctor who specializes in disorders of the newborn, from birth through the first year of life.

DISTRESS AT BIRTH—SHANNON

Kathy and Brad Leonard had been married for three years when she became pregnant. While Brad had teenagers from his first marriage, he was eager for a second family and welcomed the opportunity to take a more active part in parenting this time around.

After 18 hours of labor, Kathy's obstetrician became concerned that labor was not progressing. Since she was dilated sufficiently to deliver, he elected a forceps delivery rather than perform a Caesarean. Because the baby was not yet engaged in the pelvis, it was a high forceps delivery.

Thirty minutes after delivery, Brad was permitted to see his son. He was shocked that the baby's head was severely bruised, and that there was blood coming from his right ear. Instead of crying, Shannon was making groaning noises. Nurses were hurrying about, hooking Shannon to a ventilator to aid his breathing. When he was four hours old, Shannon had his first seizure.

Figure 4-1. Points of possible distress to the developing biological system.

DISTRESS—INFANCY AND CHILDHOOD

Most of the danger of disturbance within a child's biological system is eliminated once a normal delivery has occurred. There are a few hazards during infancy and childhood, however, which may produce a learning problem. These are described in Scipien, Barnard, Chard, Howe, and Phillips (1979). They include **nutritional deficiencies, illnesses, injuries,** and certain **medical treatments.**

Nutritional Deficiencies

Extremely rapid growth during the first year of life makes the infant especially vulnerable to shortages or imbalances in nutrient supply. By the third year, a child's brain has reached 80 percent of its adult weight. At that time, the rest of the body has only reached 20 percent of its adult size. Malnutrition during the first year of life can produce long-term intellectual deficits. While borderline deficits no doubt are also detrimental, their effects are not as easy to assess.

Illnesses

Meningitis is an inflammation of the meninges, the outer covering of the brain, and may result in hydrocephalus, mental retardation, vision and hearing defects, and seizures. **Encephalitis** is an inflammation of the brain which can cause paralysis of one or more cranial nerves, resulting in speech disorders. A **brain tumor** may produce intracranial pressure and brain damage. Hearing loss can follow **measles, mumps,** and **scarlet fever.** When **otitis media,** a middle ear infection, is chronic, it can produce mild to moderate hearing loss.

Injuries

Any accident which results in a blow to the head may produce intracranial hemorrhage and brain injury. Either a blow to the head or blunt trauma to the eye can result in **detached retina.**

Medical Treatment

High concentrations of oxygen are known to be toxic to the retina. **Retrolental fibroplasia** is seen most commonly in premature infants who have received high concentrations of oxygen for a prolonged period during the early days of life. Some antibiotics given to premature babies can cause loss of vision or hearing.

DISTRESS IN INFANCY – BRIDGET

Jan Marshall's first pregnancy was easier than she had anticipated, and so she was stunned when she went into labor at seven months and delivered a one-pound baby girl. Considering her gestation age of only 28 weeks, Bridget appeared to be a healthy baby, showing no signs of respiratory distress. She was fed through a tube to her stomach and started gaining weight.

At three days old, she developed an infection and was given an antibiotic for a period of 10 days. Bridget remained a patient in the neonatal clinic for two and a half months, and she weighed three pounds, 15 ounces when she was dismissed.

* * * * * *

In Chapter 5, we will follow Marian, Owen, Shannon, and Bridget from birth through infancy and early childhood. Of particular interest will be how their development veers from what is considered the norm. All of these children have experienced distress in the biological system. The master plan developed for each child, however, will provide for treatment at all needed levels of system.

PROMOTING WELLBEING
AT THE BIOLOGICAL LEVEL

In this chapter, we will follow the four children introduced in Chapter 4—Marian, Owen, Shannon, and Bridget—from first family awareness of a problem through eventual evaluation and treatment. As we shall see, these children will enter the health care system at different points, but, thanks to a holistic orientation of the professionals first consulted, they receive treatment at all levels of system.

MARIAN

Unsure as to whether to bring Marian home or to plan for her institutional care, the Hammonds consulted their pastor. He did not hesitate in answering their question. "All families have a special shape," he said, "yours will have a different shape from others but also special. Take Marian home so she can become part of your family."

Ruth and Guy proceeded to treat Marian in the same way they had their first daughter, Meghan, now three. Not knowing what to expect in terms of a Down child's development, expectations were laid aside, so that whenever Marian sat up or said her first word, this was considered the prime time to do so.

Daily events were used as opportunities to stimulate language. At bathtime: "Marian, find your tummy; raise your arm so Mama can wash." At breakfast: "Milk or juice, Marian, tell Daddy which one you want." Despite such attention to language development, by the age of four, Marian continued to speak in two-word combinations. While this would not be unusual for most Down children, for Marian the language delay seemed marked when contrasted with her visual-motor skills. She was already drawing circles and squares and printing her name.

At the time of Marian's routine physical exam, Ruth pointed out her apparent lag in speech development to the girl's pediatrician, and he referred the family to a developmental psychologist for evaluation.

To the psychologist, the term "Down Syndrome" implied limited intellectual functioning and consequent delays in speech, language, and motor skills. Aware that the label failed to answer other important questions about Marian, such as her special abilities and motivation to learn, she proceeded to take a case history from the family and arrange for testing.

Since Marian was diagnosed as having Down Syndrome at birth by chromosome testing, her primary disturbance was already known to be in the biological system. The first step in evaluation was to determine the relative influence of template and environment upon her ability to learn. The psychologist would attempt, by testing, to figure out as best she could Marian's innate potential to learn as represented by an I.Q. score. From her interview with the Hammonds, she would estimate the quality of stimulation provided in the home.

Marian scored in the educable range of intellectual functioning on the Wechsler Preschool and Primary Scale of Intelligence (WPPSI). She scored 14 points higher on the performance scale of the WPPSI than on the verbal scale, demonstrating her visual-motor skills to be superior to language skills.

Case history information suggested an early preference for visual stimuli. Her parents reported that she would always choose blocks, Tinkertoys®, or paper-and-pencil activities rather than having a story read to her or listening to music. In the play room, the psychologist watched as Marian played with the doll house. She put the furniture in the appropriate rooms and added the doll family members. While Marian had them interact, she did so silently with little verbalizing aloud on her part.

The data pointed to Marian's being a visual learner. Family life appeared to be maximally stimulating; however, Marian lacked outside contacts with children of her mental age. While the psychologist knew of no medical treatment for Down Syndrome, she was aware that nutritional supplements can help ready a retarded child to learn. With these facts in mind, the psychologist made the following recommendations: (1) referral to a speech-language pathologist for therapy to improve Marian's verbal communication skills; (2) half-time placement in a regular preschool in a three-year-old class; and (3) referral to a clinic specializing in vitamin treatment for the retarded. Table 5-I summarizes Marian's treatment plan.

Table 5-I
SUMMARY OF MARIAN'S EVALUATION AND TREATMENT PLAN

Primary System Disturbance:	Biological
Template/Environment:	Educable range of intelligence
	Highly stimulating home environment
Learning Style:	Looker
Treatment Plan:	Biological system — vitamin supplements
	Social system — speech and language therapy; regular preschool class

After a second evaluation, this time by a medical doctor specializing in nutrition, Marian was placed on a vitamin program. The doctor explained to the Hammonds that in some cases vitamin supplements had been shown to raise I.Q. in retarded children and bring their weight closer to the normal range by reducing the amount of fluid retained in their bodies. At age four, Marian had the typical Down shape—short, stocky, and overweight.

Following a third evaluation by a speech-language pathologist, Marian began individual language therapy. Marian's language lessons were kept in a large workbook which was sent home with her each week. Family members, housekeeper, and babysitter alike got in the habit of picking up the workbook and helping Marian add a new word to her vocabulary, learn a grammatical structure, or print a letter of the alphabet. Because of this intense work, Marian began making rapid progress in communication and pre-reading skills.

Changes in Marian were apparent after a few months of treatment. She was becoming more verbal, organizing her thoughts and

Figure 5-1. Professionals who work with handicapped children should consider keeping a resource file as an important part of their work.

expressing herself more clearly. Also, her memory was improving, and she was able to recall specific events from the past week. When her preschool teacher asked what Marian had for dinner the night before, she recalled in detail: "Turkey, dressing, rolls, salad, and peas from Mama's garden."

By the time Marian turned six, she was reading words and phrases. Her speech-language pathologist was now focusing on the concept of short and long vowels. In the fall, Marian was enrolled in a special education class in the mornings and a regular kindergarten class in the afternoons.

OWEN

When Marian was a few hours old, her parents knew that their daughter would be handicapped in learning because she was born with Down Syndrome. The Powells, on the other hand, had only a hint that there might be a problem with their son, Owen. He was

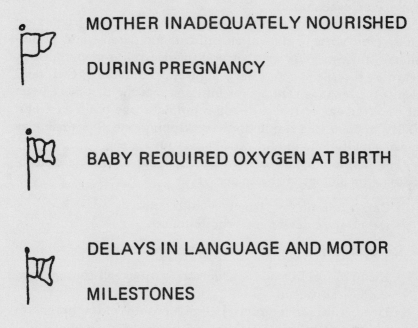

MOTHER INADEQUATELY NOURISHED

DURING PREGNANCY

BABY REQUIRED OXYGEN AT BIRTH

DELAYS IN LANGUAGE AND MOTOR

MILESTONES

Figure 5-2. Red flags signaling Owen's need for evaluation.

full term and a good-looking baby. Louise could not forget, however, that Owen required oxygen at birth, and she wondered what could have been wrong with her baby.

As an infant, Owen had feeding problems. His formula was changed several times before he was able to digest it easily. He was a placid baby and did not require the attention his two-year-old brother, Ryan, did. By temperament, Ryan was more fussy and less adaptable than Owen.

Owen cooed very little and slept a lot. He sat up at nine months and began babbling shortly thereafter. He continued to babble for a long period of time, and his first word, "mama," did not appear until he was two years old.

Owen lagged behind Ryan in nearly all areas. Careful not to compare the two boys, Louise told herself that Owen was not slow, just on his own timetable. The family doctor agreed that there was no cause for alarm and suggested that she wait another year before seeking an evaluation.

Because such a wide range of language and motor behaviors are considered normal, it is often difficult for parents and professionals alike to know at what point a referral to a specialist in learning disorders is necessary. Figures 3-3 and 3-4 in Chapter 3 depict the language and motor milestones of the first three years of life. Remember that milestones unfold as the brain develops. Delay in achieving a milestone or skipping one altogether may mean a malfunction in the central nervous system.

The developmental patterns which signal a possible disturbance to the biological system are:

- Delays in achieving language milestones.
- Delays in achieving motor milestones.

Disturbances in the biological system may be coupled with:

- Disturbances in emotional development or self-concept (psychological system).
- Disturbances in interpersonal relationships or self-help skills (social system).
- A case history event which suggests distress in the biological system (See History of a Child's Biological System, Table 5-III).

Louise was still dieting and low in energy level. While she attended to her two boys' physical needs, she did not feel up to spending much time with them. Louise found Owen to be particularly frustrating. He seemed listless and resisted her attempts to read to him or engage him in play with his toys. In the afternoons, she began leaving Owen and Ryan with a babysitter who watched television while they napped. In the evening, she put the boys in their room early so she could be alone with her husband.

When Owen entered a half-day preschool class at age four, the contrast between him and the other four-year-olds was striking. Owen was speaking in two- and three-word combinations; the other children were producing complex sentences and playing games with words. At this point, the family doctor suggested a

Table 5-II
DEVELOPMENTAL PATTERNS WHICH SIGNAL A POSSIBLE DISTURBANCE
TO THE BIOLOGICAL SYSTEM

- Delays in achieving language milestones
- Delays in achieving motor milestones
- Disturbance in emotional development or self-concept (psychological system)
- Disturbance in interpersonal relationships or self-help skills (social system)
- A case history event which suggests distress in the biological system

Table 5-III
HISTORY OF A CHILD'S BIOLOGICAL SYSTEM

PREGNANCY

Is there a history of genetic defects in the family?
Does mental retardation, learning disability, cleft palate, or any other disorder run in the family?
Is the mother older than 37 or younger than 17?
Did the mother have any infections during her pregnancy?
Did she receive adequate protein, vitamins, and minerals during her pregnancy?
Did she take any prescription drugs?
Was she exposed to radiation while pregnant?
Was this a multiple pregnancy?
Was there an Rh incompatibility?
Was the mother under stress during her pregnancy?

BIRTH

Home or hospital birth?
Was this a breech birth?
Was the baby premature?
Was the baby small for its gestational age?
Any problems with the umbilical cord?
Did the mother hemorrhage during delivery?
Was this a forceps delivery?
Was the mother given drugs during labor?
Was the birth Caesarean?
Did the baby cry at birth?
Did the baby suck readily?

INFANCY AND CHILDHOOD

Was nutrition adequate during the early years? If not, why not?
Have there been any childhood illnesses? If so, which ones?
Any recurring health problems?
Any childhood injuries? If so, describe.
What medical treatments, if any, has the child had?

referral to an interdisciplinary clinic specializing in the evaluation of learning problems in children. There were now a number of red flags, which are summarized in Figure 5-2, signalling Owen's need for evaluation.

Steve reluctantly accompanied Louise to the intake interview. He was convinced that Owen was just a bit slow in his development and that there were no serious problems. When Louise told her that Owen had required oxygen at birth, the social worker was alerted to the need for neurological testing. This was scheduled, along with psychological and educational testing.

Owen's electroencephalogram (EEG) was negative, meaning there was no evidence of abnormal brain waves. On the WPPSI, Owen scored ten points higher on the performance scale than on the verbal scale, but both scores placed him within the educable range of intellectual functioning. The psychometrist noted that Owen adapted slowly to the testing situation. He seemed to be thinking a long time before answering test questions. As a result, he lost points on timed items because of his slowness of response.

In the playroom, Owen chose the least challenging games and toys. Using the set of blocks, he built a four-block tower, and then looked to the examiner for approval. She was unable to interest him in activities requiring more skill. Owen talked very little while he played, and the evaluator noted that there was not much creativity in his play.

Because of Owen's young age, and because it appeared that he may not have had an adequate amount of stimulation at home, the psychometrist did not use the term **educable** to describe Owen's intellectual abilities. It was important now to see how far therapeutic work could move Owen intellectually. He seemed very unsure of his ability to learn, and the psychometrist suspected that Owen's insecurity was a reflection of his mother's fears regarding his development.

The psychometrist recommended: (1) Individual counseling for Louise. She seemed overly anxious about Owen's development and guilty because she could not help him herself. Because Steve refused to admit there was a problem with Owen, Louise had no one with whom to share her fears. (2) Placement in a special education preschool class for Owen. He needed work on a one-to-one basis in both language and motor areas.

Louise's anxiety about her son decreased as she talked with a psychologist weekly, and as she saw that Owen was finally getting the educational help he needed. She was relieved to see how easily the teachers worked with him, and how well he responded. As Louise's anxiety decreased, she was able to spend more time with Owen. As his mother relaxed, Owen became more relaxed, too, and more willing to attempt new tasks on his own. Repeated testing at ages five and seven bore out the original test results of educably retarded.

Table 5-IV

SUMMARY OF OWEN'S EVALUATION AND TREATMENT PLAN

Primary System Disturbance:	Biological
Template/Environment:	Educable range of intelligence
	Lacks sufficient stimulation
Learning Style:	Looker
Treatment Plan:	Psychological system—individual counseling for Mother
	Social system—special education preschool

By the time Owen was ready to enter first grade, Louise had accepted the fact that her son was mildly retarded. Having decreased her expectations, she could enjoy Owen's accomplishments. Unfortunately, it would be several years before Steve could also accept Owen's intellectual limitations. By age eight, Owen had entered a special education, first-grade class. Within a few months, he was bringing primary readers home and beginning to sound out words.

SHANNON

The day following Shannon's birth, a neonatologist and a pediatric neurologist were called in for consultation. After examining the baby, they concurred that Shannon's skull had been fractured at birth. Because Kathy was so depressed, Brad did not want her to see Shannon right away, at least not until his breathing had stabilized and he was taken off the ventilator.

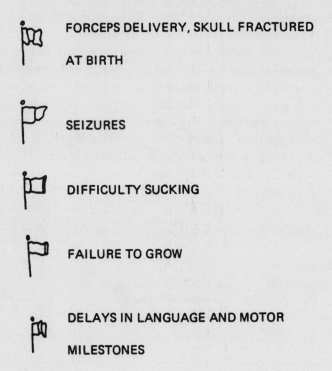

FORCEPS DELIVERY, SKULL FRACTURED
AT BIRTH

SEIZURES

DIFFICULTY SUCKING

FAILURE TO GROW

DELAYS IN LANGUAGE AND MOTOR
MILESTONES

Figure 5-3. Events in Shannon's development which confirm a disturbance to the biological system.

Three days later, Kathy saw Shannon for the first time. While his bruises had cleared up some, his head was still misshapen. It took several visits for Kathy to become accustomed to his appearance. Shannon remained a patient in the neonatal clinic until his seizures could be brought under control with medication. Kathy came to the hospital daily to be with him.

A month-and-a-half later, Shannon came home. Caring for him was trying for Kathy without the nurses' guidance and encouragement. When she held Shannon for feeding, his head flopped even if supported by her arm. Also, he had difficulty sucking. When she gave him a bottle, some of the milk drained out the sides of his mouth.

Kathy noted that the growth of his head did not keep pace with the rest of his body. By nine months, Shannon was able to sit, but only when propped. While he made some cooing sounds, he did not yet babble.

At Shannon's one-year checkup with the pediatric neurologist, Kathy expressed concern about his delayed growth and development. The neurologist now had sufficient information to make a diagnosis of cerebral palsy, mixed type. He recommended that Shannon begin physical therapy at a local hospital in the small town where they lived.

A physical therapist worked with Shannon for the next two years. By age three, he had begun saying a few single words— "mama," "dada," "light." Shannon's neurologist now recommended a complete developmental evaluation at a clinic for handicapped children in a nearby city. There he was scheduled for evaluations by a psychologist, a speech-language pathologist, and a physical therapist.

The physical therapist's findings were that Shannon's development in posture and locomotion were at about the nine-month level. He could not sit without arm support for even a few minutes. Shannon was able to pull himself to a kneeling position, but he could not cruise along furniture. When he attempted to walk with someone holding his hand, he showed a high-stepping gait. He evidenced both increased muscle tone and involuntary movements. The physical therapist recommended that pre-walking skills be the immediate goal. These included sitting, pulling to stand, and cruising. The physical therapy department fitted Shannon with short leg braces and provided a walker to assist him in walking alone for very short distances. It was also recommended that a muscle relaxant be prescribed for him in order to permit freer muscle movement.

For speech and language testing, Shannon was seated at a small table. A psychologist observed the testing through a one-way mirror. Kathy took his pacifier from him and left the room. Shannon cried for several minutes with his arms outstretched toward the door. Finally, the examiner was able to quiet him with a stuffed animal. Throughout the testing, Shannon moved about in his chair, looked around the room, and pointed to toys he wanted. When he did not get the object he pointed to, he began fussing and crying. When given a toy, Shannon pushed and pulled it across the table, sometimes putting it in his mouth, and then tossed it on the floor. Touch seemed to be Shannon's main way of interacting with the environment. When the testing was over, Shannon reached out his arms to be held by the examiner.

Testing and parent report placed Shannon's language skills at about the one-year level. He pointed to his eye, nose, and tummy on request, and when three toys were placed on the table in front of him, he followed the command, "Hand me the truck." Shannon's expressive vocabulary consisted of about ten words, including "pop," "go," "mama," "dada," and "bye." His parents reported he used words to talk about things but not to ask for them. For example, he would say "pop" if a cola drink were put in front of him, yet he would not ask for it. Instead, he would point and his parents would be left to guess what he wanted. When they guessed wrong, he would throw himself on the floor, crying.

The speech-language pathologist recommended language therapy for Shannon, utilizing the parents as his teachers. They would be taught techniques for stimulating speech development at home. The gap between Shannon's language skills and his chronological age indicated to the speech-language pathologist that Shannon was probably functioning in the trainable range of intelligence. Knowing that to call him retarded could function as a self-fulfilling prophecy, she instead spoke of Shannon's language skills as being comparable to those of a one-year-old. There was still the possibility that language therapy and increased environmental stimulation could raise his scores.

The psychologist was concerned about Shannon's behavior. It appeared that Kathy and Brad had not been firm enough with Shannon. He had learned how to control his parents without using language. Now the goal would be to convince him of the benefits of talking. In several counseling sessions, the speech-language pathologist showed Shannon's parents how to pair gestures with sounds and words, add new vocabulary, and require Shannon to use his single-word vocabulary items in appropriate contexts. Kathy and Brad realized that they had been too quiet around Shannon. They had been reluctant to use words he did not understand for fear he might become frustrated and have a tantrum. As Brad and Kathy refused to give in to Shannon's every request and required him to use language to make his needs known, the tantrums tapered off. The Leonards were linked with local community services they had been unaware of, and Shannon began individual language therapy at a cerebral palsy center in their hometown.

Intelligence testing was done yearly, and each time Shannon scored in the trainable range; however, his communication, self-help, and social skills continued to improve.

By age six, Shannon was enrolled in a full-day, special education class for trainable children. With the improvements in his communication skills and behavior, Brad and Kathy were finally able to find a babysitter who would stay with Shannon. One Saturday evening, they ventured out to their first dinner and movie alone in six years.

Table 5-V
SUMMARY OF SHANNON'S EVALUATION AND TREATMENT PLAN

Primary System Disturbance:	Biological
Template/Environment:	Trainable range of intelligence
	Lacks sufficient stimulation
Learning Style:	Mover
Treatment Plan:	Biological system—physical therapy; braces and walker; muscle relaxant
	Social system—language therapy; cerebral palsy class

BRIDGET

For the first year of life, Bridget's development seemed normal. She was about three months behind the average child on motor tasks, which could be considered normal since she had been born three months prematurely. Bridget sat up at nine months, walked with help at 12 months, and walked alone at 17 months. She was so well-coordinated, outgoing, and eager to communicate that her language lag seemed dramatic.

Bridget said her first word, "bye-bye," at 12 months. More words failed to come, and by 18 months she had stopped talking. Chris suspected she was not hearing, so he and Jan scheduled an appointment with an audiologist who specialized in testing children. While an audiogram at her age could not be exact, it did reveal a moderate, high-frequency loss. The audiologist suspected that in Bridget's case the antibiotic she had been given when she was a "preemie" may have produced her hearing loss.

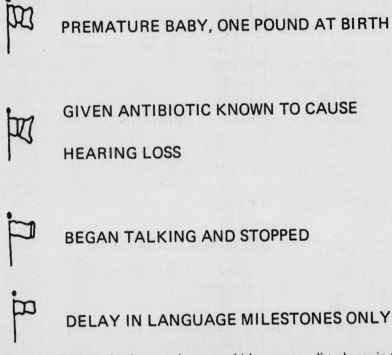

PREMATURE BABY, ONE POUND AT BIRTH

GIVEN ANTIBIOTIC KNOWN TO CAUSE

HEARING LOSS

BEGAN TALKING AND STOPPED

DELAY IN LANGUAGE MILESTONES ONLY

Figure 5-4. Bridget's developmental pattern which suggests a disturbance in the biological system.

The audiologist explained that Bridget's type of loss resulted in a distortion of the sounds she received, and that a loss which occurs in the first few years of life affects language and later academic development. He added that the fitting of hearing aids does not guarantee improved skills in communicating. Because listening is difficult, hearing impaired children often tune out auditory input and favor other input channels, so they need to be taught to tune into the auditory band of information. Because the immediate concern was the development of Bridget's communication skills, she was referred to a speech-language pathologist for evaluation.

Testing Bridget was difficult. In addition to being very young, she was very active. Her parents commented that she seemed overly active at home, and noted that she was not fearful of new situations as one might expect considering her hearing loss. The examiner observed that Bridget moved quickly about the examining room looking at the toys. She turned and watched as her parents left the room, but she did not seem concerned that they were gone. She immediately returned to the toy basket, approaching each toy in a methodical way. First, she would look each over carefully and then begin to disassemble it. She seemed very sure in using her hands. She put the rings on the spindle in sequential order and nested the cups correctly the first time. The examiner noted that Bridget did not look to her for approval, seeming to know herself when she had done something correctly. She quickly matched the geometric shapes with their slots in the shape ball, and then moved to the sand table and settled down there to play.

Testing indicated that in receptive and expressive language, Bridget was functioning much like a one-year-old compared with her chronological age of two years, two months. Observations of Bridget in play indicated that her cognitive skills were far beyond what her language skills might suggest. It was clear that her throughput, the ability to make sense of and organize incoming data, was far superior to her auditory discrimination. It appeared that Bridget had learned to efficiently process visual and tactile information to compensate for her loss of hearing acuity. The goal now would be to increase Bridget's listening skills and verbal output.

For the next year, the speech-language pathologist worked with Jan and Chris, showing them ways to encourage Bridget to listen. By age three, Bridget began individual language therapy. Emphasis was placed on teaching Bridget home, school, and food vocabulary and concepts such as **big/little, over/under,** and **top/bottom,** in preparation for a preschool class the following year. When Bridget turned four, she started attending a three-year-old regular preschool class. Because her vocabulary was very close to that of a normal, hearing three-year-old, she adapted easily. The speech-language pathologist now began teaching more difficult concepts, such as **between, far,** and **around,** ones learned automatically by hearing children without special instruction.

By the time Bridget turned four, the speech-language pathologist suggested that she be tested by a psychologist. Because of her prematurity, there was still some concern that there might be central nervous system impairment separate from the hearing loss.

The psychologist elected to use the Leiter as the primary instrument of evaluation because it contains mostly visual items and is designed to test the intelligence of children who have auditory disabilities. Bridget scored in the superior range of intellectual functioning. With this information, family, school, and therapist began to expect more from Bridget. They noted that as their expectations increased, so did Bridget's self-esteem and language performance.

Table 5-VI
SUMMARY OF BRIDGET'S EVALUATION AND TREATMENT PLAN

Primary System Disturbance:	Biological
Template/Environment:	Superior range of intelligence
	Structured, stimulating home environment
Learning Style:	Looker/Mover
Treatment Plan:	Biological system—hearing aids
	Social system—speech and language therapy; regular preschool class

* * * * * *

In Part III, which follows, we will study the psychological system. Chapter 6 covers the normal development of a child's psychological system. Chapter 7 examines disturbances which may occur at this level of system, and Chapter 8 includes the evaluation and treatment of children with psychological system disturbance.

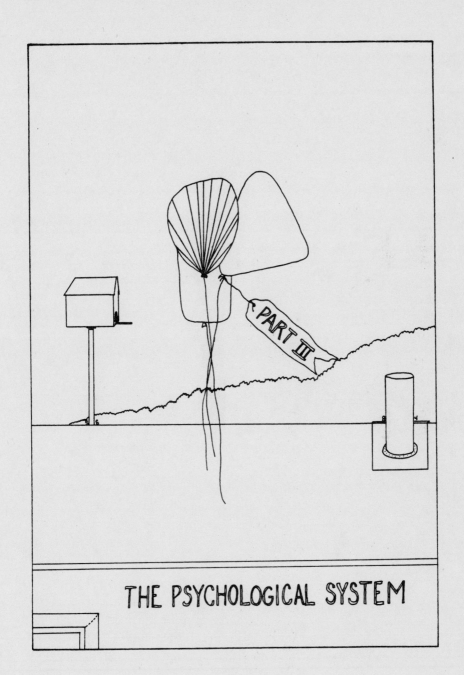

THE PSYCHOLOGICAL SYSTEM

Chapter 6

PSYCHOLOGICAL ESSENTIALS FOR LEARNING

In Chapter 3, we traced the development of Lyle's biological system from conception to birth. Now we return to look at his psychological system, which is developing concurrently with the biological. We have discussed the fact that chromosomes code for a number of characteristics, ranging from simple-to-describe ones, such as color of eyes and hair, to vastly complex ones, such as intelligence and temperament. As we shall see, Lyle's inborn pattern of temperament in interaction first with his mother, and then with the rest of the family, will lead to the crystalizing of his psychological self. Recall that the biological self is surrounded by skin. As we shall discover in this chapter, the psychological self is bounded by the **personality**.

The development of a child's psychological system may well begin before the event of conception occurs. The thoughts and feelings of the parents set the psychological climate for a baby long before it is actually conceived. The mother's concept of self is reflected in the way she cares for herself during her pregnancy and the way she responds to the life within her.

In the case of the Carters, they have been married for three years and are ready to have a child. They are emotionally and financially stable. Both have jobs they like; both plan to take part in the care of their child.

While Susan was careful to meet both the baby's and her own physical needs by proper diet, vitamin supplements, and adequate rest, she was also careful to look after their psychological needs. Susan reduced her work at the library to half time so that she would not feel stressed by her work or be too tired in the evening to spend some time with her husband. For his part, Lyle was supportive of the pregnancy and took over more of the household chores.

IN THE WOMB

Several months into her pregnancy, Susan began to experience the reality of being pregnant. She started talking to her unborn child and rubbing and patting her stomach as a means of making contact with her baby-to-be. According to Verny (1981), in his book called **The Secret Life of the Unborn Child**, memory traces begin somewhere between the sixth and eighth month in the womb. As Verny explains, "This is why what a woman thinks about her child makes such an important difference. Her thoughts—her love or rejection, or ambivalence—begin defining and shaping his emotional life" (p. 29).

Verny goes on to explain that how the fetus experiences its first world, the womb, as friendly or hostile, creates personality and character predispositions. "The womb, in a very real sense, establishes the child's expectations. If it has been a warm loving environment, the child is likely to expect the outside world to be the same. This produces a predisposition toward trust, openness, extroversion and self-confidence. . . . "

Both Lyle and Susan found themselves talking to their unborn baby. Susan often sat in the rocker in the baby's room, rocking and singing to her unborn baby, cradling him in her belly as she would later hold him in her arms. This feeling of Susan's of physical oneness with her baby will extend to a feeling of psychological oneness during Lyle's first year. Their psychological separation, which begins during his second year of life, will signify yet a second birth for him.

BIRTH AND BONDING

Susan incorporated many positive psychological benefits into the birth process itself even though she did not consciously plan it that way. In selecting a birth setting which seemed most natural and comfortable to her, she was able to relax in familiar surroundings with the people she loved about her. The Leboyer-style birth provided Susan with immediate body-to-body contact with her baby and the opportunity to breastfeed Lyle when he was just a few minutes old.

Susan had feared that if Lyle were born in a hospital setting he would be removed from her at birth and placed in a nursery. There is cause for concern over such procedures. As Montagu (1978) explains, "To remove the newborn baby from its mother and place it on its back or its front on a flat surface, often uncovered, is to fail to understand the newborn's great need for enfoldment, to be supported, rocked, and covered from all sides, and that the infant may only gradually be introduced to the world of more open spaces" (p. 233).

Klaus and Kennell (1982) have observed that mothers who deliver at home appear to be in a state of "remarkable ecstacy" which the authors call ekstasis. The feeling is contagious and the others present at the delivery often share in the festive mood. Immediately following birth to about four or five days thereafter, a sensitive period exists during which parents and child attach to each other.

To enhance the bonding experience, Klaus and Kennell recommend that mother, father, and infant have a period of uninterrupted time together of at least 30 to 60 minutes following birth. Additional intense contact among the three during the first few days after birth is also important. One time period or the other may be more important for a particular family.

Also, during the period immediately after birth, breastfeeding can begin. As Meerloo (1960) describes it, mother and baby, separated at birth, are reunited at mother's breast. This rhythmic interaction, with mother and baby clearly in tune with each other, he calls The Milk Dance. While father plays an important role in the bonding process, breastfeeding is a ritual that only mother and baby can share and that will intensify their feeling of oneness during the first year of baby's life.

Sroufe (1979) explains that baby's emotional development and attachment to Mother are intertwined. "Emotional development is intimately related to attachment, which is affective in nature, which is promoted by affective interchanges between infant and caregiver, and which has consequences for emotional growth and health" (p. 489).

Figure 6-1. The psychological system is first bounded by mother and baby. Out of their relationship, a child's personality emerges.

Baby's Temperament

Thomas (1976) and his co-workers investigated infant behaviors during the first few months of life. Brazelton (1973) focused on observable characteristics evidenced by babies in the first few days of life. He developed the **Neonatal Behavioral Assessment Scale** designed to analyze interactive behaviors through observation of the infant's first available responses to the environment. This assessment is an aid to understanding a caretaker's response to a certain child, thereby helping to predict the kind of interaction the child is likely to set up in its environment. The test includes items such as a baby's response to auditory and visual stimuli, alertness, motor maturity, cuddliness, consolability, hand-to-mouth facility, and smiling.

The categories of infant response which no doubt have a powerful effect upon the person caring for a child and, in turn, upon the child's personality, are **cuddliness** and **consolability**. The continuum of cuddliness ranges from the baby who resists being held by pushing away, thrashing, or stiffening, to the one who molds to the mother's body, leaning toward her and grasping hold. The limits of consolability range from the child who cannot be consoled even when held and rocked, to the one who is easily comforted by mother's voice and/or face.

From Lyle, Jr.'s, first day onward, he maintained satisfactory rhythms in sleeping, waking, feeding, and elimination cycles. Even more important from Susan's perspective was Lyle's readiness to cuddle. This contributed to Susan's feeling of being loved in return by her baby.

We can see from these differences in babies in terms of cuddliness and consolability that a baby has more control of the mother-child interaction than one might suspect. Granted, Susan's style of being a mother will have an impact upon Lyle, but likewise, Lyle's style of being a baby will have an impact upon Susan, and in cyclical fashion they effect one another.

Mother's Style

Escalona (1968) studied the general attributes of mother-child contacts. One variable under study was the frequency of maternal stimulation in different sense modalities which correspond to the input channels discussed in Chapter 2. Three communication bands bear information from environment to baby in the form of sounds, sights, and sensations, and these are referred to as **auditory**, **visual**, and **tactile** stimuli respectively. According to the author: "Scrutiny of all observed mother-infant contacts shows that the majority of mothers emphasize one or several modalities at the expense of others" (p. 274).

Mothers who preferred a **visual** mode of stimulation used vision as their primary or sole means of contact with their infants. A highly visual mother might smile or hold up an object for her baby to see without speaking to or touching the baby. The mothers who did not emphasize visual stimulation rarely amused their babies visually. For example, a mother not oriented to the visual mode might leave an awake and alert baby in surroundings deplete of visual stimuli, thus providing no opportunity for visual exploration.

Mothers who favored **auditory** stimulation almost always approached their babies while speaking or making humming, clucking, or blowing sounds; and they provided lots of auditory input by way of a rattle, music box, or a radio. In contrast, mothers who did not emphasize the auditory mode seldom attracted their babies' attention through sound.

The highly **tactile** mothers frequently stroked, rubbed, and patted their babies, and spent a great deal of time in play with them, providing ample holding, kissing, and tickling. Mothers not employing this mode of contact seldom touched their infants unnecessarily. They tended to keep their babies supine while feeding them, dressed them quickly, and generally held them some distance from their bodies.

Together, mother's style of stimulating, coupled with baby's inborn preference for certain types of stimuli, create a child's individual learning style.

An auditory mother, in combination with an auditory baby, will, no doubt, produce a **listener.** It is not so clear what type of learner an auditory mother and a visual baby will combine to produce. While a visually-oriented baby will seek out visual stimuli, it is still critical for Mother to see that the environment provides sufficient visual input. This may be difficult for her to do if she herself is oriented to the auditory mode. As seems to be the case with nearly every other human attribute, there are few **pure** learning types, i.e., those that are **exclusively** auditory, visual, or tactile.

Other variables observed by Escalona included intensity, intrusiveness, and competence of maternal behavior. High intensity mothers are those whose means of contact with their babies could be described as rough in nature. They are the ones who failed to shield their babies from loud noises, bright lights, or gross changes in temperature and, in fact, seemed unaware of such changes themselves. Low intensity mothers tended to be soft-spoken and to maintain a great deal of distance from their infants. Escalona cites an example of one such mother who often read a book while feeding her baby.

Intrusiveness refers to the tendency of a mother to interfere with baby's ongoing behavior, for example, rousing a baby from sleep for feeding. Mothering styles in this respect range from highly intrusive to seldom or never intrusive.

Maternal competence refers to a mother's ability to adapt to her infant's changing state. The highly skillful mothers provided head or back support when needed and gave free rein to their infants' movement impulses or restrained them playfully. At the other extreme were mothers who held their infants in uncomfortable postures, inserted a spoonful of food before their babies had finished the last, and failed to regulate their behavior in relation to their babies' present state.

Obviously, there is opportunity for quite a wide range of possibilities within these three areas of maternal behavior. The factors which would seem to be most beneficial for a child's psychological development are mother-child interaction of medium intensity, few or no intrusive behaviors, and a high degree of maternal competence. But, once again, this is highly individual and would depend upon the temperament of the baby. What seems intense or intrusive to one baby may not seem so to another baby who requires a high level of stimulation in order to experience a sensation.

Every mother-baby duo is unique. All are alike, however, in that the task of their first year together is bonding. While the achievement of psychological oneness is crucial to a baby's physical and emotional wellbeing, the actual ties that bind the two are invisible. Kaplan (1978) defines this relationship quite well:

> But for the most part the psychological forces that give a baby his human vitality are as invisible as the energies that empower him to grow and expand. The bond represents the starting point of the baby's psychological birth.
>
> To the five-month-old, the notion that either he or his mother exists

without the other is inconceivable . . . He simply has no way of envisioning himself without simultaneously conjuring some aspect of his mother—her touch, her holding arms, her smell, her eyes, the nipple in his mouth, her presence in the world (p. 121).

The bond which is initiated at birth is maintained and strengthened during infancy and facilitated by verbal and nonverbal ways of communicating.

INFANCY AND CHILDHOOD

Nonverbal Communication

The universal language of all infants is body language. A baby's readiness to touch is critical to the development of the first relationship with Mother and to the development of the psychological system. As Montagu (1978) puts it, "Touch is the parent of our eyes, ears, nose, and mouth. It is the sense which became differentiated into the others, a fact that seems to be recognized in the age-old evaluation of touch as 'the mother of the senses' " (p. 1).

Touch is probably the most important of all the dimensions of nonverbal communication and facilitates the binding together of mother and infant. As Kaplan (1978) explains: "Birth is the rupture of the state of biological oneness of mother and fetus. Mending the rupture is the major task of the mother-newborn couple. During the first month of human life mother and newborn must come to know each other in a manner that will replace the physical oneness of the womb with psychological oneness, a oneness that is as essential to life outside the womb as biological oneness was to life in the womb" (p. 59).

This constellation of behaviors which caregivers perform naturally with their babies, Stern (1977) calls "infant-elicited behaviors." As Stern explains, "Compared to most acceptable adult-to-adult social behaviors, the repertoire of a mother's actions toward her infant are quite unusual, in fact, highly deviant. They would be considered outright bizarre if performed toward anyone but an infant" (p. 10).

Stern notes that a mother's facial expressions are exaggerated in time and space when she communicates with her infant. And, while adult gazes rarely last more than several seconds, mother-infant gazes may extend to 30 seconds or more. The intimacy distance in our culture for face-to-face interaction is about two feet. Mothers readily cross these invisible boundaries with their babies.

Babies do their part to maintain the interaction with nonverbal communication behaviors of their own. At around the sixth week, the infant's visual-motor system becomes capable of visually fixating mother's eyes. The baby is able to hold the fixation with eye-widening and eye-brightening, so that the mother experiences the sensation that her infant is looking at her and into her eyes.

Some time between six weeks and three months, the smile can be brought on by outside events such as a facial expression, a high-pitched voice, or tickling. By about the third month, the smile becomes instrumental, meaning the infant will produce it in order to get a response from someone nearby. By six months, the sight of a human face or the sound of a human voice brings on the smile. By now, the baby is actively vocalizing feelings of pleasure and displeasure.

Baby Talk

In addition to acting differently with babies, adults speak differently to infants and small children than to other adults. Pitch is exaggerated, pace is slowed, sentence structure is simplified, and a **baby talk** vocabulary is used. To whom else would one say "itsy-bitsy," "choo-choo," or "potty" except to a baby?

Farb (1974) explains that baby talk, rather than representing a natural vocabulary that a child instinctively uses, actually is taught to children by adults. Baby talk is a variation of adult language, invented by adults and passed on to each generation of babies; its sole purpose being to teach children to talk. Just as children are taught to speak baby talk, they are taught to give it up once they have mastered it.

Farb summarizes studies of baby talk vocabularies in six very different cultures. While the baby talk words themselves differed from culture to culture, the themes were much the same. Almost all the words referred to eating, sleeping, and toileting, good and bad behavior, animal names, and terms for close relatives.

In general, the baby talk words were standard vocabulary, simplified. They contained easier sounds and shorter syllables, for example, "tum-tum" for "stomach," "nightie-night" for "good night," and "pee-pee" for "urinate."

It appears there are many benefits to the time-honored tradition of speaking baby talk to children. Babies get practice with simple sounds and short syllables and lots of opportunity for repetition. Perhaps most importantly, baby talk has made teaching words and learning to talk fun for generations of parents and babies.

Self-Concept

We have observed that the task of mother and baby during the first year is to bond together so that the two are physically and psychologically inseparable. There is a magnetism between them which draws and holds them together. Out of this environment of oneness, the baby flowers and grows. As Kaplan explains, "A baby's soil is his attachment to his mother. This is another way of saying that an infant's physical growth is nourished and given direction by psychological forces" (1978, p. 120). The securing of the attachment bond is prerequisite to the eventual separation of mother and child which takes place during baby's second year.

Returning to Lyle, Jr., at nine months, we find his attachment to Susan is complete. He basks in her attention, scrambling after her when she moves from his sight. Lyle will now turn when his name is called, a first step for him in developing a concept of himself. By the end of his first year, Lyle obligingly points to parts of his body—head, tummy, toes—as they are named by an adult. This feat helps to increase his awareness of self.

There are two main aspects to the developing sense of self. First is the sense of oneself as separate from other people and from objects. Next comes an awareness of the blend of traits that make each individual unique. Some of these traits are stable over time, like gender and color of eyes, and others change, like age and address.

The emergence of receptive and expressive language contrib-

BIRTH TO ONE YEAR

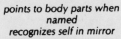

points to body parts when named

recognizes self in mirror

ATTACHMENT TO MOTHER COMPLETE

FEARS SEPARATION FROM HER

responds when name is called

VOCALIZES PLEASURE AND DISPLEASURE

smiles at human faces and voices

REACTS DIFFEREN- TIALLY TO MOTHER

smiles in response to outside events

BONDING IN PROCESS

birth	3 months	6 months	9 months	1 year

Figure 6-2. Psychological system milestones in *self-concept* and EMOTIONAL development (birth to one year).

18 MONTHS TO FIVE YEARS

MORE IN CONTROL OF FEELINGS

draws self-portrait

knows street address and town

has likes and dislikes

BEGINS TO NAME FEELINGS

uses pronouns "I" and "me"

recognizes difference between "you" and "me"

says first and last names

says "me" and "mine"

"psychological birth" is taking place

18 months	2 years	3 years	4 years	5 years

Figure 6-3. Psychological system milestones in *self-concept* and EMOTIONAL development (18 months to 5 years).

utes to the developing sense of self. Close on the heels of the first words, "mama" and "dada," are other important words, "me" and "mine." At about the same time, Lyle, Jr., begins to understand the meaning of words he hears from his mother and father which describe the kind of person they think he is or will become. Lyle is one of those fortunate children who mostly hears positives, "Good boy," "You're so smart," "How handsome you look." The words produce images in Lyle's mind which shape his emerging sense of self. The effects of such early images upon children are so long term that they reach into adulthood.

Words become associated with those most important persons who speak them, so that the words themselves take on a life of their own. "Good baby," Lyle, Jr., says when Mother is nowhere around, producing warm feelings in the absence of warm arms. Words also have a negative power, so that a critical remark spoken in anger to a child may sting every bit as much as a swat to the behind.

Susan and her baby experience a difficult period in his second year as Lyle becomes more defiant and willful. Up until this point, Susan has found comfort in her relationship with her child, but now she feels somewhat uneasy and weary because she is constantly doing battle with Lyle. According to Kaplan, "These unwelcome and frightening events are the signs that the child has at last come face to face with the decisive moments of his second birth, that he is recognizing that he is truly a separate being" (p. 34).

During this period, Lyle is intent on doing things by himself such as washing his face, cutting the meat on his plate, and putting the soap bubbles in his tub. "Me do, me do," he chants when Susan tries to help. In addition, Lyle is becoming more territorial. "My toys," he squeals as he pushes his cousin, Madeleine, away from his toy box. When things do not go Lyle's way, it is common for him to throw a tantrum or swat at his mother.

Up until this time in his life, Lyle has relied almost exclusively upon interactions with his mother and father to provide good feelings about himself. Now, using Mother as home base, Lyle carefully ventures out to explore his world. Hanging onto his mother's skirt with one hand, he reaches toward Muffin, the neighbor's dog, with the other. In a moment of bravery, he reaches out and ruffles the dog's fur and then goes squealing back to his mother.

More and more miniadventures will follow as Lyle gains confidence in himself and his surroundings. This newfound sense of independence makes for good feelings about himself. By the end of his second year, Lyle has learned to say his first and last names; holds up two fingers to show his age to inquiring adults; and can be riled up if called a girl, because he now knows he is a boy.

From age two to three, Lyle learns further attributes about himself and begins to identify with the man he was named for. Comments heard from relatives and friends such as, "You're the spitting image of your dad," and "Look how he uses his hands, he's going to be an artist just like his father," intensify the boy's identification with Lyle, Sr.

As his language skills improve, Lyle learns labels for his feelings which help him distinguish different emotional states, so that he begins to tell when he is happy, angry, or sad. Also, he learns that it is okay to say he's mad but not to pinch Madeleine or to hit a grownup, and that no situation calls for spitting.

By the time he starts to preschool, Lyle knows all the digits of his phone number, his street address, and the town he lives in, "Okamana (Oklahoma) City." In the morning before preschool, Susan usually lays out two shirts and lets Lyle pick the one he would like to wear with his jeans. One morning he chooses the blue shirt with orange stripes his grandmother gave him for Christmas. "That's a good choice," Susan says, "You look good in blue." Because he is allowed to make choices at home, Lyle is becoming aware of his personal likes and dislikes and of his individuality. By the time he begins kindergarten, he has a strong concept of self. His emotions are much more under control now, and the temper tantrums of old are nonexistent.

After about the age of five, drawings children make of human figures, trees, and houses can be used as indicators of their self concept. According to DiLeo (1973), a well-adjusted child will "draw freely, with joyful abandon, creating a figure that expresses, by its size, sweep and conspicuous placement on the page, freedom from inhibiting anxiety" (p. 36). In their drawings, well-adjusted children tend to picture themselves as feeling happy and as involved in positive actions such as going to school, playing with a friend, or helping around the house.

Figure 6-4. Children's drawings are indicators of their self-concept. Well-adjusted children usually picture themselves as feeling happy and as involved in positive actions. Ann, age 6, is cleaning the barn.

Spontaneous crayon drawings by well-adjusted children usually contain trees full of leaves and color, houses with curtains and people at the windows, and a sun in the sky reflecting the warm, nurturing environment they have experienced at home.

When the mother-baby relationship is healthy, baby emerges as an autonomous psychological system. The personality of a child is a reflection of inborn temperament coupled with interaction patterns of mother and baby. By school age, a child's personality is a cluster of feelings, attitudes, goals, and values unique to him or her.

Allport (1961) emphasizes that personality is well-knit enough to qualify as a system. Royce (1982) lists the characteristics which personality has in common with other living systems. The psychological system, or personality, has specific goals, processes information, interacts with other systems, faces uncertainties and risks, and undergoes development over the course of its life span.

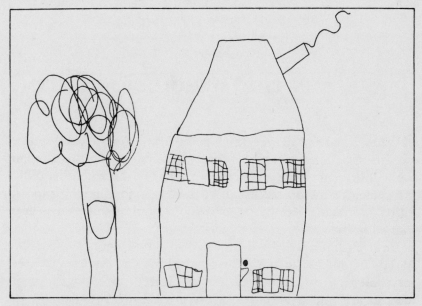

Figure 6-5. The houses drawn by well-adjusted children are usually inviting. This one was drawn by Lauren, age 6.

* * * * * *

As we have seen in this chapter, both the linking of mother and baby and their mutual letting go of each other are critical to the development of the psychological self. In Chapter 7, we will look at examples of mothering styles and babies' temperaments which are so extreme that they disrupt the normal development of the psychological system.

Chapter 7

DISTRESS IN THE PSYCHOLOGICAL SYSTEM

Baby Lyle has had everything going his way in the development of his biological and psychological systems. In this chapter, we will investigate ways distress can occur in the unfolding of the psychological system. As usual, we must keep in mind the impossibility of tracing handicaps to specific points which have been passed in time.

Four children will be introduced who represent four possible points of distress to the psychological system. As we shall see, psychological milestones are not as clearcut as biological ones, and so are not as easy to observe. While the boundary of the biological system is the skin, which can be seen and touched, the boundary of the psychological system is the intangible personality.

Children whose primary disturbance is in the psychological system will not necessarily be placed in classes for the emotionally disturbed, because disturbances which originate in the psychological system can, in turn, damage the developing biological and social systems. The educational diagnoses of children with primary psychological system disturbances may include emotionally disturbed, mentally retarded, speech and language disordered, and learning disabled.

Table 7-I

EDUCATIONAL LABELS OF CHILDREN WHOSE PRIMARY DISTRESS
IS TO THE PSYCHOLOGICAL SYSTEM

Emotionally Disturbed
Mentally Retarded
Speech and Language Disordered
Learning Disabled

106

Conception marks the beginning of the biological system. The origins of the psychological system can be traced even farther back to the attitudes and feelings of the parents before the moment of conception.

According to Verny's (1981) findings, from about the sixth month in the womb a baby can hear and record mother's and father's voices, perhaps even conversations, and can sense maternal feeling states.

We learned in Chapter 4 that a woman who experiences emotional stress during her pregnancy can, in turn, produce negative biological effects upon the child she is carrying. Stress during the first trimester can result in ill health for her baby, mental retardation, and even physical malformation. When the stress is localized to the latter months of pregnancy, her baby may be irritable, hyperactive, and have feeding problems.

Remember that the womb is the child's first world and that personality and character predispositions can be set here. Verny (1981) believes: "If that environment has been hostile, the child will anticipate that his new world will be equally uninviting. He will be predisposed toward suspiciousness, distrust, and introversion. Relating to others will be hard, and so will self-assertion" (p. 50).

One of the greatest stresses for a pregnant woman is for the baby's father to be neglectful or physically abusive of her. A father's support is "absolutely essential to her and, thus, to their child's well-being" (Verny, 1981, p. 30). The sounds of parents' quarreling linger in a baby's memories.

A child who is unwanted at the time of conception is usually unwelcomed at birth. Psychological distress ongoing in the womb culminates at birth in the disruption of the bonding process.

DISTRESS – BIRTH AND BONDING

Ideally, mother, child, and father can spend private time together immediately after birth and in the days that follow. Mother and baby require face-to-face interaction time in order to become familiar, each with the other.

The bonding process may be disrupted either because of problems within the mother, baby, or both. Some factors present at birth that are associated with failure to bond are an **emotionally disturbed mother, a handicapped child, a premature baby,** and **a baby whose temperament fails to encourage the bonding process.**

Emotionally Disturbed Mother

As Bowlby (1973) explains, a mother can be physically present to her child, but emotionally absent. A mother overwhelmed by intrapsychic conflicts has little energy available for her newborn baby. She may be too preoccupied with herself to be concerned for her child's wellbeing or with building a relationship with baby. Such a mother may be depressed, out of touch with reality, rejecting, or indifferent toward her baby. In extreme cases, a mother may feel as if she is the baby, desperate herself for nurturing.

The fate of emotionally disturbed mothers is described quite well in **Mentally Ill Mothers and Their Children,** by Grunebaum, Weiss, Cohler, Hartman, and Gallant (1975):

> The new relationship between mother and infant is particularly vulnerable to the mother's sense of dissatisfaction and failure in other aspects of her life. Withdrawal, emotional detachment, intense involvement marked by inconsistency and impulsiveness, poor judgement in evaluating the baby's needs, and seemingly irreconcilable conscious or unconscious negative feelings toward the baby—one or several of these elements may characterize the mother's behavior during her breakdown. Underscoring these reactions is her conscious awareness of extreme and inexplicable displeasure in caring for her baby; she senses her failure. (p. 85)

Handicapped Child

During the course of a normal pregnancy, parents develop a mental image of their baby-to-be. This image may be so specific as to include sex, temperament, and color of skin, hair, and eyes. While all parents are faced with resolving the discrepancy between the idealized image held in their minds and the actual appearance of their baby, the task is much greater when the baby is born with a handicap.

Klaus and Kennell (1982) outline the stages which occur in parents after they have been told that their child is handicapped. First is shock and denial, followed by sadness, anger, and anxiety, and finally a lessening of feelings and a reorganization. The authors emphasize that our society has no customs, traditions, or rites to support parents when they have an abnormal baby. Parents are unsure whether or not to send birth announcements. Friends do not know whether to visit or to allow the parents to be alone.

Stern (1977) explains that parents are both biologically and culturally predisposed to respond to the features of a normal newborn, to its facial configurations and behaviors. When a baby is born with some type of disformity, especially one which disrupts the configuration, parents tend to hold themselves back from fully reaching out to their infant.

In order to ease the acceptance of a handicapped child into a family, Klaus and Kennell recommend that the mother not be tranquilized and that she be allowed to see and hold her baby as soon as possible. Usually, the actual appearance of the child is not half so frightening as the imagined one. At the parents' first encounter with their baby, the doctor or nurse present can take this opportunity to emphasize positive features of the child, such as strength, alertness, or activity level. An added help is for a special nurse to be assigned to the mother to be available for extended periods of listening and giving comfort.

Premature Baby

A baby born prematurely is separated from its mother and placed in a special care unit as quickly as possible. This separation from the mother is as much a threat to the baby's wellbeing as any physical disorders it may have.

Parents should be permitted to see their premature baby as soon as possible and should be forewarned that the baby's appearance may be frightening. The parents' first view will be that of a scrawny little baby surrounded by wires, tubes, and bandages, and enclosed in an incubator, physically inaccessible to them. Like the parents of a handicapped child, the parents of a premature baby must reconcile their idealized image of a healthy, robust baby with the one actually present before them.

Klaus and Kennell (1982) caution doctors about making pessimistic remarks in the first hours of a premature baby's life. Such remarks may cause the baby's mother to hold back, thereby stifling the development of the bond between them. Pessimistic remarks so early on may result in the mother's beginning a process of anticipatory grief. Once a mother has begun to mourn even the imagined loss of a child, it may be nearly impossible for her to reverse the process.

The authors recommend that the mother of a premature baby be permitted inside the nursery and be allowed to caress and hold her child on a daily basis. Even within this artificial environment, she can begin to build her relationship with her child and come to feel competent in her ability to care for her baby. This fact will be particularly important when the time comes for the baby to go home.

Baby's Temperament

Babies whose temperament could be a problem may be recognizable from the first day of their lives. These include babies who will not cuddle, are difficult to console, lie passively, resist being held, or are very irregular in sleeping, waking, and feeding cycles. A baby whose behavior is far from the norm, coupled with a mother who requires a great deal of feedback in order to perform her mothering role, can result in the failure of bonding to take place.

Extreme types of temperament disorders such as autism or childhood schizophrenia may rupture the mother-child bond even when the mother is experienced and nurturing. A mother who habitually gets no feedback from a listless baby or receives negative feedback in the form of crying, screaming, and kicking when she attempts to handle her child, may lose interest and come to reject the baby, either consciously, unconsciously, or both. Since temperament disorders become more apparent during the course of infancy, they will be discussed in more detail under the heading, **Infancy**, later in this chapter.

The first child representing distress in the psychological system is Claire. Her problems are confounded from the start because she has also experienced distress in the biological system.

DISTRESS IN BONDING—CLAIRE

Claire is a full-term baby born to Maryanne and Roger Cooper, a young couple who live in a small rural town in Ohio. Maryanne and Roger had both graduated from high school a few months before Claire's birth, and Roger had just started his first job selling farm equipment. They were totally unprepared for the birth of a baby with a cleft lip and palate.

Maryanne had a difficult pregnancy. She had gotten married because she was pregnant, and she wasn't sure she wanted to be married, let alone have a baby. There were wedding showers and baby showers, and she began to get excited about fixing up the house she and Roger were renting and decorating the baby's room.

When the doctor told her that her baby had been born with a cleft lip and palate, Maryanne immediately thought about her college-age cousin who had a thin line of a scar on his upper lip, the only remaining evidence of his "hare lip." When the doctor asked if she knew what cleft lip meant, Maryanne nodded. She was still thinking of her cousin when the baby was brought to her.

Maryanne began crying hysterically when she saw her baby. Claire's lip and palate had not yet been repaired, although surgery was scheduled for the following day, and her appearance was shocking. Neither Maryanne's parents nor her husband could comfort her. She cried intermittently during her stay in the hospital and for weeks after she returned home. Her mourning for the baby of her dreams seemed endless, and Roger could not console her. Maryanne refused to go and see Claire while she was in the hospital recovering from surgery. Maryanne's mother checked in on her granddaughter daily, confident that Maryanne would accept her baby now that the cleft had been repaired and her appearance was improved.

DISTRESS IN INFANCY—ATTACHMENT

When normal bonding progresses, a mother attaches easily to her child as she gets to know the qualities which make this baby unique. In the early days and months, a mother will be affected by the temperament of her baby. Of equal importance is the mother's personality, flexibility, self-concept, and the amount of encouragement she requires from her baby in order to mother.

Most babies accomplish their attachment to Mother by eight months. Babies who fail to attach in the first year of life later show effects in three main areas. Fraiberg (1977) describes these as: 1) varying degrees of impairment in the capacity to attach themselves to substitute parents or to any persons; 2) impairment of intellectual functioning during the first 18 months of life; and 3) disorders of impulse control, particularly in the area of aggression (p. 53).

It is assumed that babies have indeed attached when they can be observed crying and following after Mother when she leaves, moving toward and clinging to her when alarmed, and smiling differentially at Mother.

Remember that it is the mother-child relationship which forms the boundary for the psychological system. Mother has the primary role in the development of her child's psychological system; father's role is of secondary importance. As Mahler, Pine, and Bergman (1975) explain: "Father as a love object, from very early on belongs to an entirely different category of love objects from Mother. Although he is not fully outside the symbiotic union, neither is he ever fully part of it" (p. 91).

Some of the factors which affect the process of attachment in the first year of life are **overstimulating mothers, understimulating mothers, emotionally disturbed mothers, difficult babies,** and those with **autism** or **childhood schizophrenia.**

Overstimulating Mothers

These are the mothers who bombard their babies with more stimuli than they can comfortably take in at a given time. Stern (1977) refers to such mothers as exhibiting a "chase-dodge" pattern, the mother chasing, the baby dodging to avoid the stimulus overload. Such mothers seem to be unaware of their child's comfort state and continue to stimulate even when the child is not showing interest or is actively avoiding the incoming stimuli. As a defense measure, the overstimulated child may shut down one or more input channels. Mother-child interactions such as these could result in a learning disabled, language disordered, or emotionally disturbed child.

Understimulating Mothers

Mothers in this category fail to reach their babies' threshold of stimulation, perhaps because they themselves are chronically depressed, apathetic toward motherhood, or because their babies require a stronger type of input stimuli than they can provide. Such mothers show a lack of energy, expression, and enthusiasm when relating to their babies. Such children may later receive educational labels such as mentally retarded, learning disabled, language disordered, or emotionally disturbed.

Emotionally Disturbed Mothers

While it is relatively easy to question a new mother regarding how she experiences her baby, one can only imagine how an emotionally disturbed mother may seem from her baby's perspective. Imagine looking into eyes that reflect indifference or even hate, or being held in lifeless, uncaring arms. Some children of emotionally disturbed mothers are lucky enough to have a sister, grandparent, or other relative who can supply some degree of emotional warmth and affection.

According to Grunebaum, et al. (1975), an emotionally disturbed mother adversely affects her child by giving inadequate physical care, being withdrawn emotionally, and by providing "erratic, contradictory, insufficient, or overwhelming stimuli" (p. 198).

Extreme cases can result in a **reactive attachment disorder of infancy.** Onset is before eight months of age and is characterized by lack of visual tracking of the eyes, weight loss, weak cry, excessive sleep, lack of smiling in response to faces, and a general lack of interest in the environment.

Children of emotionally disturbed mothers may themselves become emotionally disturbed, or they may be mentally retarded, language disordered, or learning disabled.

Difficult Babies

Some babies may be difficult to handle in the first few months and then finally make some sort of adjustment to the routine of family life. Other difficult babies grow into difficult children. Their sleeping and waking cycles fail to regulate, their aversion to touch does not subside, and their activity level remains intolerable. Such children are in danger of becoming rejected or even injured by their own families. According to Korner (1979), the statistics on battered children point to the "prevalence of unrewarding, difficult babies among those who become victims of child abuse, sometimes even at the hands of different sets of caregivers" (p. 775).

Autism

The onset of autism is usually before 30 months. One of its chief characteristics is a profound failure to relate to other people. This failure to relate is often apparent at birth. The social smile is usually absent or delayed, and the impairment in language acquisition is dramatic. As a rule, these children do not make use of gesture to communicate their needs, and seem to be deeply embedded within themselves.

The autistic child shows either an underresponsiveness or an overresponsiveness to touch, light, sound, and pain. Affect is inappropriate, so that the child giggles, laughs, or cries uncontrollably. The autistic child shows obsessive, ritualistic behaviors characterized by staunch resistance to change; for example, demanding one type of furniture arrangement or one type of food, at times to the point of becoming hysterical if anything is changed (Koegel, Rincover, and Engel, 1982).

Childhood Schizophrenia

The child who will be later diagnosed as schizophrenic may or may not be identifiable at birth. These children are often very appealing as babies. Only after they are brought home does the schizophrenic pattern begin to emerge.

As infants, they show poor muscle tone which keeps them from molding to their caretakers. They may hang limply or stiffen when held. Some are fearful and irritable from the beginning, and most display sleep disturbances.

As babies, they have what Cantor (1982) calls "remarkable visual attentiveness" which may lead parents to think their child is very bright. Babbling usually does not appear until the end of the second year. Lacking words, these children communicate their needs by pulling and gesturing. Typically, their language functioning is much higher than that of autistic children.

Perseveration is typical, evidenced by repetitive actions or sticking to an activity once begun or to a toy. They may display mannerisms such as hand flopping, rocking, head banging, and pacing.

Schizophrenic children seem to have a marked inability to screen out irrelevant sensory stimuli. As Cantor explains, "Every sound, smell, and sight strikes this child with equal intensity" (p. 32). It is common for them to prefer numbers, letters, and noiseless machines, such as calculators, to toys of any kind. In later childhood, schizophrenic children may be plagued by delusions, hallucinations, and loosening of associations not experienced by autistic children. Autistic and schizophrenic children most often end up in classes for the emotionally disturbed or mentally retarded.

DISTRESS IN ATTACHMENT – TRAVIS

Travis was the third male child born to Margaret and Joe Hanson. Since Joe's promotion to fire chief, the Hansons had decided that they could afford one more child to complete their family. The birth was easy, and the baby was beautiful.

Margaret noted the first time she held Travis that he did not feel like her other boys. His body would tense up when she held him and would relax when she put him down. After a few days, Travis quit tensing up when held, but now felt "like a dishrag," as Joe described the way his son lay in his arms.

Margaret reminded herself daily not to compare Travis to the other boys, that he had his own special personality. Her husband repeatedly pointed out how bright Travis must be because he was so visually alert. He would stare at a mobile above his crib sometimes for hours, never seeming to tire.

By the end of the first year, Travis was making no attempt at talking. Motor milestones were on target, so Margaret tried not to concern herself too much with the language delay. While Travis had a playpen full of toys, he preferred to play with his dad's calculator. He would sit for long periods pushing buttons and watching the screen light up, oblivious to the goings on about him. When not occupied with a favorite object, Travis would flap his hands or twirl. Margaret tried to limit this kind of activity by leaving him with his calculator as long as he wished.

Travis never seemed to get days and nights straight. He slept often during the day and was awake most of the night. Margaret and Joe became so accustomed to this behavior that they forgot that most children do not behave this way. Exhausted, one day Margaret confided to a close friend what they had been going through. Her friend urged Margaret to consult with a child psychiatrist who had helped her son with a school phobia. When Margaret told her family doctor that she planned to have Travis evaluated, he said she was an overanxious mother and suggested tranquilizers for her.

DISTRESS IN INFANCY – SEPARATION

Some time during the second year, mother and baby begin a pulling apart, which is essential for the wellbeing of each. In this way, the infant begins to form an identity, a sense of self separate from Mother. When this process is not resolved, disturbances in the psychological system result.

Symbiotic Psychosis

In extreme and rare situations, an infant may remain fixed at a state of psychological oneness with Mother. In such cases, the child's sense of personal identity is absent. Factors which may contribute to the development of symbiotic psychosis in a child are an extended illness, an overload of environmental stimulation, and unpredictable mothering which typically involves a pattern of overstimulation followed by abandonment.

Separation Anxiety

This refers to the excessive anxiety experienced by a child following separation from a parent. Children with this condition tend to be preoccupied with thoughts of loss of their parents through death. They often have difficulty going to sleep, experience a fear of the dark, and have physical complaints such as stomachache, headaches, or nausea. Separation anxiety often develops after a life stress, such as the death of a relative or pet. Children manifesting symbiotic psychosis or separation anxiety usually receive the label, emotionally disturbed.

SEPARATION DISTRESS—JENNY

Jenny was a full-term baby born to Lenore and Sam Rossi. While they had known each other for many years, their marriage was not stable. Lenore had hoped a baby might draw them closer together.

The baby thrived and seemed a bit ahead of schedule in all developmental milestones. Close relationships developed between Lenore and Jenny and Sam and Jenny, but Lenore and Sam's relationship with each other did not seem to improve.

Sam, a salesman, spent less and less time at home. When Sam was home, he and Lenore quarreled often, usually about money. By the end of the baby's second year, Lenore was feeling happiest when Sam was not home. One spring, he made a business trip to Atlanta, and Lenore did not hear from him again.

Lenore simultaneously felt relief that the quarreling was over and anxiety because now she had to provide full support for herself and Jenny. Lenore took a job nights as a waitress and left Jenny in her sister's care.

During the daytime hours Lenore spent with Jenny, she often felt tired or preoccupied. Jenny seemed to become more and more irritable, cried easily, and repeatedly asked where her Daddy was. When Lenore was called to fill in for a sick employee during daytime hours, the extent of Jenny's anxiety became apparent for the first time. When Lenore returned home several hours later, the babysitter reported that Jenny had cried off and on during the entire time she had been gone and could not be comforted. After that day, Jenny would not let Lenore out of her sight. When Lenore went to the mailbox or to answer the phone, Jenny clung to her skirt, and she refused to sleep in her own bed.

DISTRESS IN CHILDHOOD

Psychological distress may have its inception at early stages of development and not surface until the childhood years. A psychological disturbance ties up the child's energy with emotional conflicts, energy that might otherwise be directed toward learning.

When the primary disturbance is in the psychological system, it may manifest as either a biological, psychological, or social disorder, or a combination thereof. Following are just a few examples of disturbances within these three categories. The terms used are from the Diagnostic and Statistical Manual of the American Psychiatric Association (DSM-III) (1980).

Biological

These are the psychological disturbances which manifest through the physical body. **Obesity** is a condition of being overweight when no physical reason can be found. **Enuresis** refers to a repeated involuntary urination during the day or night past the age when bladder control is expected. **Encopresis** is an involuntary passage of feces at inappropriate times and places.

Psychological

In these cases, the outlet for a psychological disturbance is the psychological system itself. For example, an **overanxious** child shows unrealistic worry about future events and overconcern about competence in a variety of areas—academic, athletic, and social. Such a child may also have physical complaints such as headache or stomachache. **Depressed** children are those who show a lack of affect, loss of energy, and preoccupation with self. Children with a psychologically-based **learning disability** are those who early in life were either bombarded with stimuli so that they shut down one or more input channels, or, conversely, who were inadequately stimulated.

Social

These include the disorders that manifest as disturbances in social relationships, either because of excessive withdrawal or acting out. Children who display a schizoid disorder are characterized by a defect in the capacity to form social relationships. Such children show no interest in making friends and may actively avoid all nonfamily contact. Elective mutes display a continuous refusal to speak in almost all social situations, including school. Typically, they are able to understand verbal language and to speak, but choose not to. The undersocialized child with a conduct disorder habitually violates the rights of others. Such a child fails to establish a normal degree of affection, empathy, or to bond with others, and shows a lack of concern for the feelings and wellbeing of others. Children with an oppositional disorder are disobedient, negativistic, and provocative toward authority figures.

DISTRESS IN CHILDHOOD – DYLAN

At the time of Dylan's birth, his mother was involved in a drug community in Los Angeles. While Sara refrained from taking drugs during her pregnancy, she resumed the habit after her baby's birth. Sara supported herself and Dylan with odd jobs, living from week to week. The two lived in a rundown house with several other families. There was little routine to their lives, and people moved in and out of the home daily. Sara was caring and playful with Dylan when straight, and unavailable when stoned.

When Dylan was four, Mickey moved in with them and referred to himself as Dylan's father. Mickey was an explosive person, yelling and throwing things when angered. Several times Dylan saw his mother pinned in a corner or yanked by the hair, and once he saw her threatened with a kitchen knife. Dylan prayed that Mickey would die.

One day, returning home from a nearby park with several other children, Dylan saw an ambulance in front of his house. His

Figure 7-1. Points of possible distress to the developing psychological system.

mother, in tears, was being led out by a police officer. The first thought that raced into Dylan's mind was: "I killed him."

* * * * * *

In Chapter 8, we will follow Claire, Travis, Jenny, and Dylan from the time of their psychological evaluation through the treatment process. We will note how their development veers from the norm and the early indicators of emotional disturbance. While the primary system disturbance for all children is the psychological, their master plan will, of course, provide treatment at all levels of system which require it.

Chapter 8

PROMOTING WELLBEING
AT THE PSYCHOLOGICAL LEVEL

In this chapter, we will follow the early lives of Claire, Travis, Jenny, and Dylan. Recall that each child's primary disturbance is within the psychological system. This disturbance, however, may express as a lag in biological, psychological, and/or social development. Psychological milestones are perhaps the most difficult to observe and document, because they are mostly internal to the system.

In the children which follow, we will find:
- Emotional instability.
- Lag in the development of self-concept.

Disturbance in the psychological system may be coupled with:
- Delays in language and/or motor milestones (biological system).
- Disturbance in interpersonal relationships or self-help skills (social system).
- A case history event which suggests distress in the psychological system (See Table 8-II, History of the Psychological System).

Table 8-I
DEVELOPMENTAL PATTERNS WHICH SIGNAL A POSSIBLE DISTURBANCE TO THE
PSYCHOLOGICAL SYSTEM

- Emotional instability
- Lag in the development of self-concept
- Delays in language and/or motor milestones (biological system)
- Disturbance in interpersonal relationships or self-help skills (social system)
- A case history event which suggests distress in the psychological system

Table 8-II
HISTORY OF A CHILD'S PSYCHOLOGICAL SYSTEM

PREGNANCY

Mother's emotional health during pregnancy?
Was baby planned?
Is mother in stable relationship with baby's father?

BIRTH

Home or hospital birth?
Was mother sedated?
Was child premature or handicapped?
If hospital birth, did baby "room in" with mother?
Were mother and baby able to spend private time together during the hours following birth?
Was baby breast or bottle fed?

INFANCY AND CHILDHOOD

Was baby cuddly?
    liked to be held?
    wanted to be alone?
    smiled readily?
    easy to console?
    alert?
How do mother and child interact?
What is mother's learning style?
Could baby have had too much or too little stimulation?
Does attachment appear to have taken place?
If child is of preschool age, does he/she separate easily from mother?
Does child refer to self by name? Use personal pronouns?

CLAIRE

Claire stayed in her grandmother's care for several weeks following surgery. The baby's appearance was much improved, and Mary hoped that her daughter would find Claire more acceptable now.

At one month of age, Claire was moved from her grandmother's to her parents' home, and Maryanne reluctantly accepted the change. While she routinely met her baby's physical needs, Maryanne could not make herself reach out to Claire in a warm way. There was little face-to-face contact between the two. Feeding was slow because of Claire's struggle with sucking, so Maryanne often read a paperback while feeding her baby.

Maryanne spent part of the grocery money Roger gave her each week for babysitters. Practically every afternoon, she would meet her old high school girl friends for a coke, leaving Claire with a babysitter. Ashamed of her baby's appearance, she did not want to take Claire along. On her afternoons out, Maryanne did her best to forget that she was a mother.

Mary made it a point to stop by to see her daughter, son-in-law, and granddaughter no more than once a week. She was convinced that the three of them needed time alone to come to feel like a family. Maryanne was only too happy to let her mother fuss over the baby and care for her during her visits.

By the time Claire turned one year old, Mary began to take note of how little time mother and baby were together. Maryanne would leave Claire in her playpen for long periods. At the end of the first year there were no words, and Claire showed no interest in walking.

As Mary noted the lags in Claire's development, she began to think that maybe she had been wrong to insist that Maryanne care for the baby when her heart was not in it. Her granddaughter's mental health suddenly seemed more important than her physical handicap. Mary insisted that the baby be taken to a local mental health center for evaluation. Not quite understanding the concern, Maryanne and Roger nevertheless agreed to the evaluation.

Mary accompanied her daughter and son-in-law to the initial meeting. She talked with the social worker first to provide some background information. Mary explained that at age 18 Maryanne was not emotionally prepared for either marriage or motherhood. She told about Maryanne's reaction when she saw her baby for the first time. Her mother noted that while Maryanne did not cry openly any more, she still seemed to be deeply depressed.

While Mary talked with the social worker, a developmental psychologist tested Claire, using the Denver Developmental Scale. The psychologist asked Maryanne to hold Claire while items from the Denver were administered. Some items required Maryanne to tell whether or not she had observed Claire perform in a certain way at home.

Besides crediting Claire with a pass or fail on each item, the

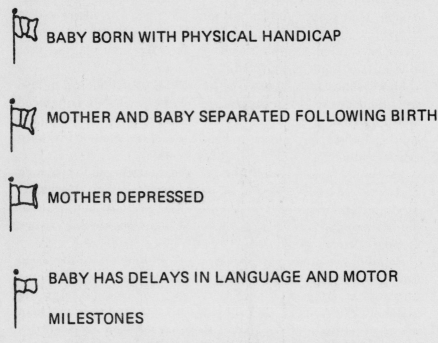

Figure 8-1. Red flags signaling Claire's need for evaluation.

psychologist noted the interactions between mother and baby. Maryanne gave little attention to Claire. She did not encourage her or reward her for responding.

When Mary, Roger, and Maryanne met with the social worker for the test results, they were told that there were lags in Claire's development in all areas tested—fine and gross motor, language, and social skills. Claire was not receiving sufficient stimulation at home in the form of auditory, visual, and tactile input. At this point, delays were mild, and there was no reason to think Claire's intelligence was impaired.

While Maryanne did not understand the meaning of the words, the implication was clear to her—she had not been a good mother to her baby. At that point, Maryanne broke down and cried. She had tried not to think about Claire for so long, hoping the problems would just go away, but now she could not avoid thinking any longer.

The social worker had two immediate recommendations. They were: 1) individual counseling for Maryanne, and 2) therapy twice a week for Claire with a child development specialist. It was suggested that both Maryanne and Roger come for the session with the child development specialist who would model ways to stimulate Claire's development. Until now, Roger had taken little part in child care, and both Claire and Maryanne needed his participation.

Maryanne looked forward to her sessions each week. After several months of talking with the social worker, she opened up her feeling of disappointment regarding the birth of her baby and was surprised to find her therapist could readily understand her feelings. Because cleft lip and palate could be found on Maryanne's side of the family, she and Roger agreed to see a genetic counselor before having any more children.

Maryanne enjoyed watching the child development specialist play with Claire, seeing how easily and quickly Claire responded. For the first time, Maryanne could see how bright her baby was, and she began to enjoy the give-and-take of play and feel proud of Claire's accomplishments. Roger took time off from work each week to go with Maryanne. She was pleased to see Roger playing with his daughter for the first time.

A secondary surgical procedure was performed when Claire was two-and-a-half, and this improved her appearance even more. This time, Maryanne was able to lend emotional support to her child and roomed in with her at the hospital. There she met two other young mothers who were dealing with the same problem. Following the surgery, Claire's communication skills were evaluated by a speech-language pathologist. Receptive and expressive language skills were at age level, so therapy was not recommended, but a reevaluation in one year was suggested.

When Claire turned three, she began a half-day preschool class. At the same time, Maryanne took the first job she had ever had, a half-time one at a local flower shop.

Table 8-III
SUMMARY OF CLAIRE'S EVALUATION AND TREATMENT PLAN

Primary System Disturbance:	Psychological
Template:	Probably normal range
Environment:	Severe lack of stimulation
Learning Style:	Impossible to tell at this stage; baby has not had sufficient stimulation for any input channel
Treatment Plan:	Psychological system — individual therapy for mother
	Biological system — secondary surgical procedures and genetic counseling
	Social system — work with child development specialist; evaluation by speech-language pathologist; regular preschool placement by age three

TRAVIS

Travis was evaluated at a much later age than Claire, even though his delays were more marked. Margaret continued to extend her timetable for concern: "I'll worry if he isn't talking by 18 months. . . . by two. . . . by two-and-a-half. . . . " and so on.

She held on to the name and number of the child psychiatrist, secretly hoping she'd never have to call him. After five sleepless nights in a row, she decided to call Dr. Samuels; just to get some sleeping medication for Travis, she told herself.

Margaret made the first appointment without telling her husband. She decided to tell him later, once she had confirmed that there was nothing wrong with Travis. Dr. Samuels listened thoughtfully as Margaret talked about her son. She described the way Travis stiffened when held, or hung limply in her arms; his sleeplessness at night; his language delay; and his outright refusal to play with anything but his dad's calculator. Margaret suddenly felt silly. All told, these behaviors did not seem so bad, and she said so to Dr. Samuels.

His response was not what she expected. He assured her that she was not being silly, and that there was reason for great concern. He urged Margaret to bring Travis in as soon as possible and made an appointment for him the following day.

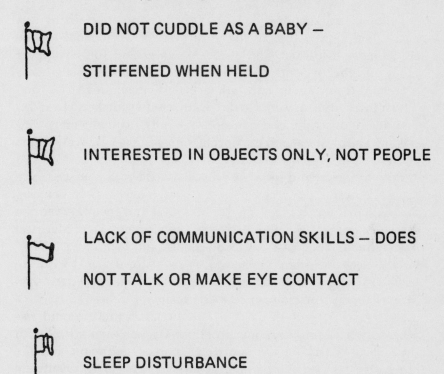

DID NOT CUDDLE AS A BABY —

STIFFENED WHEN HELD

INTERESTED IN OBJECTS ONLY, NOT PEOPLE

LACK OF COMMUNICATION SKILLS — DOES

NOT TALK OR MAKE EYE CONTACT

SLEEP DISTURBANCE

Figure 8-2. Concerns of Travis's family in regard to his development.

Dr. Samuels spent a half hour in play with Travis. He noted Travis's hand-flapping, his lack of speech and eye contact, and his pulling and tugging of Dr. Samuels's arm to get an out-of-reach toy. He asked a colleague, a clinical psychologist, to administer the Wechsler. The psychologist found Travis to be virtually untestable. Dr. Samuels insisted that both Margaret and her husband be present for a discussion of his findings.

Margaret was surprised by Joe's eagerness to accompany her to the psychiatrist's office. Dr. Samuels explained that case history information, coupled with observation and testing of Travis, revealed a pattern of characteristics which, together, are referred to as **childhood schizophrenia**. He told them that while the etiology of the disorder is not known, a number of kinds of treatment have been found to be helpful.

Dr. Samuels recommended: 1) a private clinic specializing in a nutritional approach to mental disorders, 2) a preschool for the emotionally disturbed, and 3) for Margaret and Joe, a support group of other parents of schizophrenic children. He suggested that they think about and talk over his recommendation and return in a couple of weeks to discuss the matter further. He added that, like most childhood schizophrenics, Travis had widely contrasting abilities, some in the normal range, some below, and some above.

Both Margaret and Joe were overwhelmed by what needed to be done and hesitant to accept the diagnosis. There was no denying the diagnosis was correct the day Margaret and Joe observed the preschool class Dr. Samuels had recommended for Travis. Margaret was stunned to see five boys who looked and behaved a lot like Travis. Each little boy seemed to be in his own world with the teachers trying to coax him out. Margaret and Joe agreed to begin Travis's therapy program as soon as possible.

First, Travis went through a nutritional evaluation and was placed on a vitamin-mineral program. He was then enrolled in the special preschool five mornings a week. Margaret and Joe regularly attended the parents' group. Joe's fireman's insurance allowed both Margaret and Travis to see Dr. Samuels for a one-hour session each week.

By age four, improvement was evident. Travis was speaking in four- and five-word sentences and making eye contact. Having met several teenage schizophrenics through the parent group, Margaret and Joe had come to realize that Travis was dealing with a lifelong disability. They learned to be thankful for small increments of progress. Now that Travis was sleeping through the night, family life was much improved. Tears came to her eyes when Margaret saw her three boys playing catch together in the backyard. It was the first time Travis had been included.

JENNY

When Jenny was three years old, Lenore changed to working days and put Jenny in a daycare center. Parting each day was traumatic. The first week Jenny cried intermittently every day

Table 8-IV
SUMMARY OF TRAVIS'S EVALUATION AND TREATMENT PLAN

Primary System Disturbance:	Psychological
Template:	Uneven abilities, some in normal range
Environment:	Easily overstimulated, needs special program to facilitate learning
Learning Style:	Looker
Treatment Plan:	Biological system—vitamin therapy
	Psychological system—individual therapy for Travis and his mother
	Social system—special preschool class, parent support group

and could only be quieted for short intervals of play.

After a week, Jenny still had not settled down, and the director of the daycare center realized that this was not the usual case of adjustment. At the end of this first week, the director told Lenore that they could not keep Jenny unless Lenore agreed to talk with a family counselor.

Lenore immediately agreed. She knew they needed help. She signed a release form permitting Mrs. Finley, a social worker who consulted with the center, to observe Jenny during the day. What Mrs. Finley observed was a child unduly stressed by separation from her mother. The day Mrs. Finley visited the center, Jenny cried and called "mama" for over two hours after her mother left. She stayed to herself on the playground and in the classroom and would not join the children in play, preferring to hang on to her teacher's hand and watch from afar. Mrs. Finley's recommendation was that Lenore and Jenny come for a complete evaluation at the mental health center where she was employed.

While Dr. Frank, a clinical psychologist, tested Jenny, Mrs. Finley interviewed Lenore. Lenore talked about the stress she felt during her pregnancy because her husband did not want the responsibility of a child. Jenny had been a very easy baby who was doted on by her father; while he enjoyed playing with her, he did not want to take part in her care.

Jenny had received lots of input from both parents in the form of sights, sounds, and touch. Baby liked to be held, was easy to

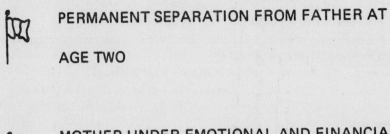

PERMANENT SEPARATION FROM FATHER AT

AGE TWO

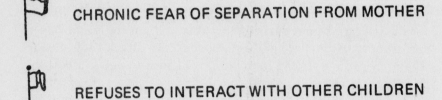

MOTHER UNDER EMOTIONAL AND FINANCIAL

STRESS

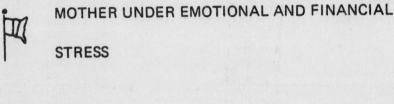

CHRONIC FEAR OF SEPARATION FROM MOTHER

REFUSES TO INTERACT WITH OTHER CHILDREN

Figure 8-3. Signs of disturbance in Jenny's development.

console, and was very affectionate. Jenny smiled at three months
and began to walk and talk before one year. Lenore described
Jenny's development as "supernormal" until the time Sam left.
That had been over a year ago, and they had had no word from
him. For the first time, Lenore admitted how deserted by her
husband and smothered by Jenny she had felt.

Meanwhile, Dr. Frank was attempting to test Jenny. After a
half-hour of crying for her mother, Jenny finally fell exhausted to
the floor. Eventually she noted the large toy box beside her and
slowly began to investigate its contents. She readily engaged herself in play with noisemakers, blocks, and crayons. Jenny found a
book on a low shelf, brought it to the examiner, and asked to be
read to. She sat next to Dr. Frank on the couch with her head
against his shoulder while he read to her. Afterward, she agreed to

sit at the little table and chairs and was administered the Peabody Picture Vocabulary Test.

The psychologist's testing and observations of Jenny revealed bright-normal intelligence and an equal facility in processing stimuli in all input channels. He interpreted his findings to Lenore and explained that because of the closeness of the relationship, Jenny was experiencing Lenore's anxiety, as well as mourning the loss of her father. Jenny was afraid that Lenore would also go away and not come back. He suggested: 1) individual therapy for Lenore, and 2) Parents Without Partners as a way to meet other single parents.

The daycare center agreed to take Jenny on a three-month trial basis, and at the end of that time to reevaluate whether or not Jenny had made an adjustment. But, by then, progress was evident. Both Jenny and Lenore were more relaxed, and separation was easier. Lenore found she was both better able to enjoy the time she spent with Jenny and to be more available to her.

Table 8-V
SUMMARY OF JENNY'S EVALUATION AND TREATMENT PLAN

Primary System Disturbance:	Psychological
Template:	Bright-normal range of intelligence
Environment:	High level of multi-channel input
Learning Style:	Looker/listener/mover
Treatment Plan:	Psychological system—individual therapy for Lenore
	Social system—Parents Without Partners

DYLAN

After Dylan's mother was taken to jail, he was placed by the county in a local foster home until arrangements could be made for him to move to his grandparents' home for an indefinite stay. They lived in a small town in a neighboring state; both were in poor health. Because Sara had not been on good terms with her parents, Dylan had seen his grandparents only twice. His stay in the foster home marked the first time he had been away from his mother, even for an overnight stay.

The summer with his grandparents seemed like a vacation. Dylan helped his grandparents in the field, went fishing, and fed the farm animals. Since this time felt like a holiday, Dylan expected to return to his mother and to start first grade back in Los Angeles.

In September, Dylan was enrolled in first grade in a small nearby town. A school bus picked him up daily at the mailbox. Dylan's grandmother went with him for the first day of school. He felt funny having her there. She looked so old compared to the other boys' mothers. His teacher, Mrs. Brandon, was young, like his mother, and he liked her right away.

Each evening his grandparents asked if he had any homework, but Dylan said no. After supper he spent the evening watching television. Dylan would have preferred to play softball, but his grandfather, because of his arthritis, did not feel up to playing.

At the end of the first nine weeks, Dylan's grandmother received a gradecard covered with minuses, along with a note asking her to come in for a conference. Mrs. Brandon reported that Dylan was picking fights on the playground and was having trouble with his schoolwork. He was steadily falling behind the other children in reading. His grandmother signed the permission slip so that Dylan could be evaluated by a psychologist from a local guidance center.

The testing revealed a learning disability in the auditory area, explaining Dylan's difficulty in learning phonics. His scores on the WISC–R were: Verbal Scale, 85; Performance scale, 95. When asked to draw a person, Dylan drew a boy on top of a house standing next to a chimney: "The little boy feels tired climbing that mountain. He is smelling the food coming out of the chimney, and waiting for an airplane to come and take him down." Dylan's drawing made clear the emotional ordeal he had been through.

When the psychologist interviewed Dylan's grandparents, he asked for developmental history and found that they had no information to give him. They explained the kind of lifestyle their daughter had lived and their estrangement from her.

The recommendations made were: 1) one-to-one work with a learning disability teacher at school to help Dylan catch up with

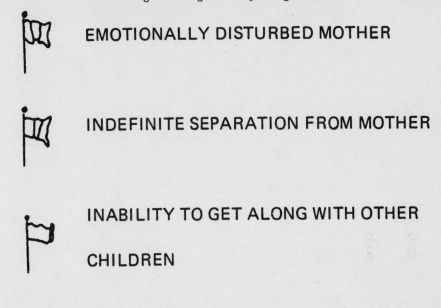

EMOTIONALLY DISTURBED MOTHER

INDEFINITE SEPARATION FROM MOTHER

INABILITY TO GET ALONG WITH OTHER

CHILDREN

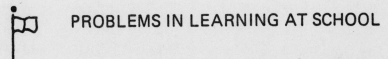

PROBLEMS IN LEARNING AT SCHOOL

Figure 8-4. Indicators of disturbance to Dylan's psychological system.

his class; 2) individual psychotherapy for Dylan on a weekly basis to give him an opportunity to work out his feelings about his mother; and 3) enrollment in a Big Brother program sponsored by a local men's club.

Shortly after the evaluation, Dylan' mother was sentenced to six years in prison for manslaughter. This meant that Dylan would be living with his grandparents indefinitely. They knew that because of their age and health they were not able to function as parents for him and needed all the outside support available.

Dylan worked with a tutor during the summer months, and by the time he started second grade he had almost caught up with his class. He was now on a Little League softball team, and he had joined a Cub Scout troop. His Big Brother saw to it that he made practice sessions and meetings.

Figure 8-5. Dylan's self-portrait—"The little boy feels tired climbing that mountain."

The clinical psychologist who worked with Dylan could see growth. Dylan was talking more and hitting less. More problems lay ahead, however. Sara had asked to see her son at Christmas, and a decision needed to be made whether or not to allow Dylan to visit her in prison.

Table 8-VI
SUMMARY OF DYLAN'S EVALUATION AND TREATMENT PLAN

Primary System Disturbance:	Psychological
Template:	Normal range of intelligence
Environment:	May have experienced both over- and under-stimulation in infancy
Learning Style:	Looker/mover
Treatment Plan:	Psychological system—individual counseling for Dylan
	Social system—learning disability tutor; Big Brother program

* * * * * *

In the next section of the book, we will study the social system. In Chapter 9, we will look at the normal development of a child's social system; in Chapter 10, investigate disturbances which may occur at this level of system; and, in Chapter 11, follow evaluation and treatment of children with social system disturbances.

Chapter 9

SOCIAL ESSENTIALS FOR LEARNING

In Chapters 3 and 6, we were onlookers to the unfolding of Lyle's biological and psychological systems. Returning once again to Baby Lyle, we will now watch his social system evolve. At the moment of birth, fetus becomes baby and enters its first social system—the family.

Let's review what we have learned thus far about a child's systems and their boundaries: The biological system is surrounded by skin and is the physical body; the psychological system is bounded first by mother and baby and later by the personality.

Social systems can be likened to a pebble dropped into a pond. They form an everwidening circle of reference for the individual. As we discussed in Chapter 1, the unit of the social self is the **role**. From sociology we learn that the role, rather than the individual, is the smallest unit of a social system, and that **role** refers to the expected behavior of an individual in a group setting. The social systems which Lyle will be a part of are first, his family; later, his neighborhood, school, and community.

In the early months of Baby Lyle's life, Susan and Lyle, Sr., are probably not as aware of their baby's social self as they are of his biological and psychological selves. Lyle's little physical being demands constant upkeep and care. He must be fed and diapered at regular intervals. Any irregularity in the ticking of Lyle's biological clock alarms the family unit. If he is unable to sleep, if he is unusually fussy, or if he refuses to nurse, his mother and father respond with concern.

Susan is also very much in tune with Lyle's psychological self. While she is not consciously aware that she is part and parcel of his psychological system, she does intuitively sense a oneness with her baby. Susan learns to anticipate Lyle's needs, becoming nearly

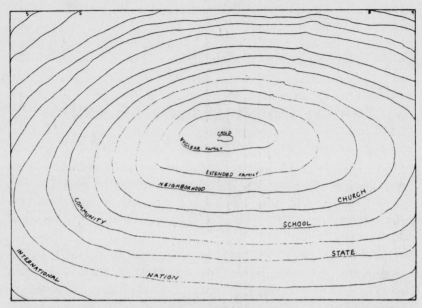

Figure 9-1. Social systems are like a pebble dropped into a pond. They form an everwidening circle of reference for the individual.

as sensitive to his body signals as she is to her own. Susan craves physical closeness with Lyle, as does he with her, and there is a feeling of rightness for Susan when her baby is in her arms.

BIRTH THROUGH INFANCY

In the first few weeks following birth, Susan and her husband spend equal amounts of time with their son. Lyle, Sr., takes off a six-week summer session from teaching to be at home with Susan and the baby. He needs time to try out his brand new role of father, unhindered by what could be conflicting role demands at work.

The period of bonding has often been described as if it were exclusively for mother and baby. It is interesting to note that Klaus and Kennell's first book on bonding was entitled **Mother-Infant Bonding** (1976). Their revised edition of that book has been retitled, no doubt to reflect the recognition of the importance of father in the bonding process, and is called **Parent-Infant Bonding** (1982).

Elkind (1981) points out that only in the past decade have we come to understand how much even young children are attached to their father and how vital this attachment is to their healthy growth and development. Elkind says: "In part this may be because contemporary fathers are likely to be more involved in child care than in the past and to feel more comfortable in the nurturant role. But fathers were probably always more important to children than was thought in the past (p. 152)." Throughout this chapter, we will periodically refer to a father's impact upon different aspects of his child's social development.

Lyle's relationship with his mother and father are vital to the development of his social being. His parents' relationship with each other also influences his social development. As we shall discover, anything which affects one member of the family affects all, because the family is a system.

FAMILY AS SYSTEM

During his first weeks at home, Lyle is repeatedly welcomed into the family. Grandparents, aunts, uncles, and cousins stop in to meet the newest member of the family. Each of these persons will play parts of varying importance during Lyle's growing years. Role requirements will eventually reach beyond the nuclear family as Lyle takes on the roles of son, boy, grandson, nephew, and cousin. It will be a number of years before he takes on yet other roles of friend, schoolmate, and pupil.

While it may seem obvious that Susan and Lyle, Sr., have assumed the roles of mother and father, respectively, it is not so obvious that Lyle is in the process of taking on the role of baby and is beginning to act, at least to some degree, in accord with parental expectations. As Kaye (1982) explains, mother and infant "do not begin to be a social system until the infant, too, has expectations of how the mother will behave. These must be expectations based on experience together, not genetically programmed information like the expectations spiders have about the behavior of flies" (p. 35).

For there to be a role, there must be two persons who hold expectations for one another, because roles are based on "reciprocal

Figure 9-2. The family is the boundary of a child's first social system.

behavioral expectations" (Carlile, 1980). A Lyle, Sr., requires a
Lyle, Jr. Father and son roles are complementary and necessary to
each other. Other roles which interlock are mother-baby, husband-
wife, and sister-brother.

When Baby Lyle enters the family at birth, he does not immediately become a fully functioning member. In the early months,
when mother and baby are still one, they make up a subsystem of
the family system. It is only after Lyle accomplishes his second,
psychological, birth that he can become a member in his own
right. As Kaye (1982) explains: "The infant first is differentiated
from the maternal system that gave birth to him—a psychological
process lasting some months after the physical severing of the
umbilicus—and then he gradually is attached to the parents'
preexisting social system as an individual member" (p. 226). Since
the family operates as a system, all roles are interdependent, as
Watzlawick, Beavin, and Jackson (1967) explain: "The behavior of
every individual within the family is related and dependent upon
the behavior of all the others" (p. 134).

Parsons and Bales (1955), in a classic text on the family, make a distinction between the roles of mother and father. In general, it is father who links the family to society as a whole, and mother who acts as caretaker of the family system. According to the authors, "the mother role tends to be anchored between family and mother-child systems, the father role more between family and extra-familial systems" (p. 81). The two roles are referred to as "expressive" and "instrumental," respectively.

For the full, healthy functioning of the family system, both roles must be played effectively. As we shall see when we examine the changing American family, expressive and instrumental roles are not as clearly defined as they were in the 1950's when Parsons and Bales wrote their book.

Now we turn to look at Lyle's early life in the Carter family.

FAMILY LIFE

Susan and Lyle, Sr., have found it very easy to adjust to their baby; it is doubtful they suspect that he has also found it quite easy to live with them. The baby's sleeping, waking, hunger, and elimination cycles are regular and so are his parents' responses to them. Family life is orderly and predictable.

Lyle, Sr., returns to his teaching at the end of the summer. He leaves for work and returns at about the same times each morning and afternoon. The baby internalizes the rhythm of his father's coming and going, and can anticipate when it is time for Daddy's return from work.

When Lyle gets hungry, he is fed. While feeding, Lyle spends long periods of uninterrupted time with the love of his life, his mother. Susan often puts on a favorite folk song album from her college days as background music for her baby's dinner. Their home is filled with pleasurable sounds, sights, and smells. Susan takes Lyle into the kitchen with her while she is preparing dinner, and he usually accompanies her on at least one outing a day—to the grocery store, post office, or bank.

Before putting Lyle to bed, his father holds and rocks him. Sometimes he sings old favorites that were sung to him by his mother and father when he was a child. These songs produce warm feelings within him, and he communicates these to his baby. "Rock-A-Bye-Baby," "Here Comes Santa Claus," and "Swannee River" sound equally good to his audience of one.

By three months of age, Lyle's smile becomes a social phenomenon because it can now be brought about by environmental events. He shows his social self in other ways as well. When Aunt Irene leans over his crib and tells him he is a beautiful baby, Lyle stops cooing until his aunt has finished talking, and then begins to coo again, never missing a beat in the give-and-take of conversation. As Sherif and Sherif (1956) explain, "Social life is the natural habitat of the human individual" (p. 8).

By the middle of Lyle's first year, he is taking part in games with his parents. While he does not yet have the words for Pat-a-Cake, he does have the moves and squeals down pat. Demonstrating some independence, Lyle is now reaching for crackers and cookies and feeding them to himself. By nine months, he's drinking from his own cup, and at one year he delights in pulling off his own socks. By now, Lyle knows the meaning of the dread word, "NO!" and responds appropriately. When first words emerge, Lyle gleefully discovers that "wahwah" sends his Daddy-Giant running for a cup of water.

Note that through Lyle's interactions with his social and physical environment, he is receiving ample stimulation in all three input channels—auditory, visual, and tactile. We've seen that a child comes to favor one or more input channels as a result of inborn preferences in combination with the types of stimuli available in the early environment.

Occupations often reveal learning styles. Susan is a librarian, and Lyle, Sr., is an art teacher. She is a looker/listener; he is a looker. Despite their own input preferences, they are aware of the need to supply multi-channel input for their baby. Lyle eventually settles into a looker style of learning, probably due to the force of his genetic predisposition inherited from both parents.

Of the three types of input, the tactile is probably most important for social development. Montagu (1978) explains that early tactile stimulation is critical to a child's ability to establish contact relations with others later in life. He says: "Unlike vision or hearing, in contact we feel things inside us, inside our bodies"

(p. 101). He adds: "Hence touch is not experienced as a simple physical modality, as sensation, but affectively, as emotion. When we speak of being touched, especially by some act of beauty or sympathy, it is the state of being emotionally moved that we wish to describe" (p. 103).

Lyle's early tactile experiences with both mother and father have been warm and inviting. Because of these experiences, one would expect Lyle to grow into a warm, responsive person himself and to be capable of forming positive relationships with others and being a loving parent in turn.

No doubt some might think that Lyle has been born into the "ideal" family. His physical, emotional, and social needs are being well met; in addition, his family is intact and living under one roof. This type of family grouping has typically been thought of as the "average American family." In fact, there are fewer and fewer such units, and some authorities believe that the average American family is dying.

Levine (1978), however, suggests that the family in America is not dying, but, rather, changing, and that children and adults need support in coping with that change. He says: "We can start offering that support by laying to rest the myth of the average American family. In its place, we can begin acknowledging—in our classrooms, in our primary school readers, on our TV shows—the existence, strength, and variety of the many families in which children actually live" (p. 14).

Rather than the ideal family being synonymous with an intact unit, Satir (1972), a family therapist, suggests that an ideal family is a healthy one. A family can be healthy whether it is a two-parent family, a one-parent family, or what Satir calls "blended families," those that are step, adopted, or foster. Remember that from a systems perspective, all of these are family systems because they are portions of the world perceived as a unit and able to maintain their identity despite changes.

Satir calls families "peoplemakers." Children enter the family system (by birth, by adoption, or for foster care), and, when the atmosphere within the family is right, they exit as healthy individuals. In the healthy families Satir has observed, she finds "self-worth is high; communication is direct, clear, specific, and honest; rules are flexible, human, appropriate, and subject to change; and the linking to society is open and hopeful" (p. 4).

As Lyle enters his preschool years, his parents will have plenty of opportunities to demonstrate how firm, yet flexible, they can be.

PRESCHOOL YEARS

Month by month, Lyle is changing, as he accomplishes biological, psychological, and social milestones and moves on to more. The milestones include language and motor development, self-concept and emotional development, and self-help and social skills. Being the **looker/listener** that she is, Susan most enjoys interactions with Lyle when language is involved. She reads to Lyle daily, and they play listening games, like "Who Can Hear the Postman First?" She praises all his efforts at communication, ignoring any production problems he may have, such as saying, "dow" for "cow." Lyle points out pictures he likes in old catalogues, and his mother cuts them out. On rainy afternoons, they paste the pictures in a scrapbook and tell stories about them. In this way, Lyle rapidly adds new vocabulary, like "margarine," "camper," and "girdle."

Lyle, Sr., a **looker**, focuses more on visual input and fine motor activities with his son. He joins Lyle in Tinkertoy and block play and in making castles in the backyard sandbox.

Just before Lyle turns three, his parents succeed in toilet training him. It is a difficult time for all of them. Until this point, Lyle has responded to internal signals for the timing of biological functions. Now, he is being required to eliminate at socially-approved times and places. Lyle resists, but ultimately he yields to family pressures.

When he is three, Lyle is old enough to take part in a morning preschool class at a neighborhood church. This marks his first "ecological transition," Brofenbrenner's term for "shifts in role or setting which occur throughout the life span" (1979, p. 3).

Until now, Lyle's interactions have been mostly with members of his nuclear and extended family. His playmates have been his cousins, Madeleine and Carl, in addition to a few neighborhood children. Preschool is Lyle's first experience in a group other than his family. The preschool group is made up of 12 three-year-old boys and girls and two teachers. We say that Lyle is "in" the group. However, to be in a group—that is, located within its boundaries— does not mean the individual is entirely engaged by it (Cartwright and Zander, 1968). The role an individual plays within a group is determined by group norms and values which serve as a coding device that allows more or less of the person "in."

Lyle's fit in his classroom system is like that of a hand in a glove. His social characteristics match the dimensions of the group almost exactly. Like the other children, Lyle is middle class, his parents are professionals, and he lives in the same neighborhood of two-story, well-kept houses. In Chapter 10, we shall see that problems arise for children for whom there is not such a comfortable fit between individual and group.

True to form for a system, when one member makes a change, all are affected in some way. Lyle's entrance into preschool precipitates changes within the family. Susan now has mornings free to enroll in a graduate class in library science. During the evenings, she goes to the library to do research for the paper she is writing; Lyle, Sr., stays home to babysit. He fixes dinner for his son, and they spend the evening together. This is the most active Lyle, Sr., has been in his son's care since the summer of his birth. This has positive benefits for Lyle's developing sex-role identification.

MALE-FEMALE IDENTIFICATION

The attainment of a child's sexual identity comes about as the result of the interaction of many factors. These include a child's biological predisposition, the mother-child relationship, and influences from society by way of the family, peers and school experiences.

Satir (1972) stresses that both parents are necessary for a child's development of sexual identity. When a parent is absent from the home (because of work demands, separation, or divorce), more often than not it is the father.

After the psychological birth from mother is complete, boys and girls begin to identify with the parent of the same sex. Because fathers are usually away from home during the day, they "are a more ambiguous and less accessible sex-role model for their sons than mothers are for their daughters. As the young boy shifts from mother-identification and searches for a new model, the father's warm participation in his care may be especially important" (Lynn, 1974, p. 160).

Current societal definitions of **masculine** and **feminine** are in transition. May (1980) believes that one fruitful way to think of male and female differences is in terms of degree of differentiation and separateness. As he explains: "Again and again male events partake of moving away from, of separating oneself from the context, of pushing off and out into space. Female events are more akin to being part of, staying in touch with, being embedded in" (pp. 110–111).

This definition parallels that of Parsons and Bales (1955) describing the role played by mother and father within the family. We might summarize these observations by saying: Maleness is a link; femaleness, an anchor.

One way children practice sex roles is through play.

PLAY

Through play, children explore the surrounding world, gain knowledge, release emotions, and learn to interact with others.

Toys have always been a primary focus of children's play. At one time, many toys were considered to be either boys' toys or girls' toys. Trucks and a catcher's mitt were for boys; dolls and dishes for girls. When children themselves are permitted to pick their toys, the choices are sometimes surprising. Lyle, at three, likes to rock and bathe his doll as much as his cousin, Madeleine, does. She, in turn, enjoys playing "highway" with toy trucks and cars. When the two play house, Madeleine sometimes dresses up like a "mommie" and other times like the "milkman." Lyle sometimes is "daddy" and other times is the "Avon lady." When children play house, some favorite home life themes are packing, taking a trip, shopping, cooking, dining, and repairing—often with no particular differentiation as to sex of the participant.

While Susan and Lyle, Sr., continue to be aware of the need to provide multi-channel inputs, they are also careful not to over-load the child-system. Rather than overstimulate Lyle with too many toys, they buy only a few and make many of their own at home. From their own childhoods, they recall the fun they had hitting spoons on pans, stacking metal measuring cups, and put-ting a doll to sleep in an oatmeal-box cradle.

Parents play an important part in giving permission for chil-dren to fantasize during play. With such encouragement, play leads to a rich life of fantasy. When Lyle, at four, puts on a cape to play Superman, Susan says, "You can fly through the air and jump over buildings. Superman can do anything."

Pulaski (1974) emphasizes the importance in a child's life of the ability to fantasize: "Clearly, make-believe play is an intrinsic part of normal growth. It is associated with verbal fluency, waiting ability, increased concentration, positive attitudes in life, flexibility, originality, and imagination" (p. 74).

To sustain an active life of fantasy, children need privacy and quiet time to make up their own games, stories, and characters—time unhindered by the "canned" fantasy of television, movies, and video games.

SCHOOL YEARS

After being a preschooler for two years, Lyle finds the transi-tions to kindergarten, and then first grade, quite easy to make. He has internalized the ways children-in-classrooms behave. As Bird-whistell (1970) points out, exactly how social norms and values are internalized remains a mystery.

Lyle's first grade teacher notes quite a contrast between Lyle (and other children like him who have learned to play the role of student) and the two Indian children in her class. The Indian children, in school for the first time, are unused to a classroom setting and have never before interacted with white middle-class children or adults.

By first grade, Lyle is fully immersed in the culture of childhood. He knows the language, dress, and behaviors that allow him to fit in. Beginning in his preschool years, he learned to play tag, and to be "it" without complaining. He learned that boys his age like jeans, not shorts or dress pants. And he knows that "step on a crack, break your mother's back!"

As Lyle will find, in first grade there are new rules to learn and challenges to be met. In this more structured school setting, there is increased emphasis on mastery and on striving for competence. The boys on his block begin to show an interest in who can run the fastest, who is the tallest, and who is the strongest.

T-ball, which has been played in backyards, is given up as the boys learn softball and soccer and play scheduled games on school-yard fields. Along with the cheers, uniforms, and teams with names, comes a feeling of competition that Lyle has not experienced before.

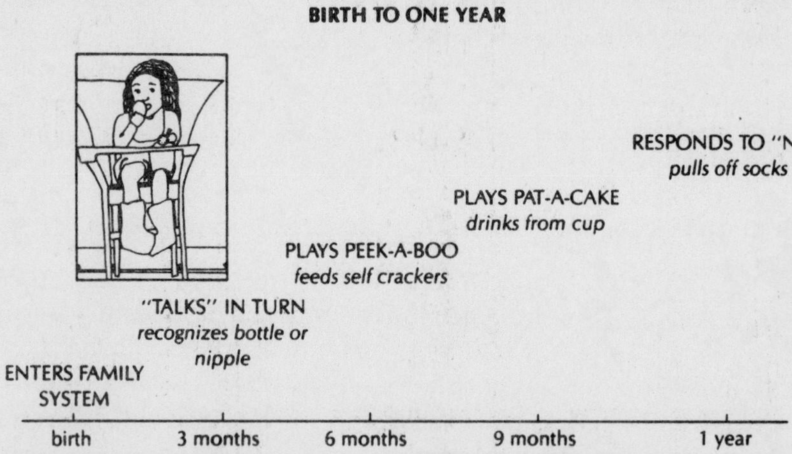

BIRTH TO ONE YEAR

RESPONDS TO "NO"
pulls off socks

PLAYS PAT-A-CAKE
drinks from cup

PLAYS PEEK-A-BOO
feeds self crackers

"TALKS" IN TURN
recognizes bottle or
nipple

ENTERS FAMILY
SYSTEM

| birth | 3 months | 6 months | 9 months | 1 year |

Figure 9-3. Social system milestones in **self-help** and INTERPERSONAL development (birth to one year).

Also, for the first time, Lyle senses competition at school. Pre-school and kindergarten work had come easily to him. But when reading is taught in first grade, Lyle finds he does not quite understand what is expected and cannot easily commit to memory the sounds required for reading. Since Susan is a combination visual and auditory learner, she not only can empathize with

18 MONTHS TO FIVE YEARS

PLAYS SIMPLE
TABLE GAMES
dresses alone

SHARES
buttons and unbuttons

PLAYS HOUSE WITH
OTHER CHILDREN
toilet trained (boys)

PLAYS NEAR OTHER
CHILDREN
toilet trained (girls)

IDENTIFICATION
WITH PARENT OF
SAME SEX
uses spoon, spills little

| 18 months | 2 years | 3 years | 4 years | 5 years |

Figure 9-4. Social system milestones in *self-help* and INTERPERSONAL development (18 months to 5 years).

Figure 9-5. Rudy, age 9, pictures the members of his family sitting together watching "Happy Days" on television.

Lyle, she can also provide him the auditory information he is lacking. She takes time after school to show him how visual and auditory units relate. "See," she explains, "these are two letters, c and h, but together they make one sound—hear it? It sounds like someone is sneezing." The association is made, and after a faltering start, Lyle takes off and begins reading.

By school age, children's drawings of the human figure reflect self-image. Their drawings of family members reveal what family life is like for them. Children from healthy families often show family members taking part together as a unit in activities such as eating, playing a game, or watching television. Mother, the nurturer, is often shown in the kitchen preparing a meal; father, working around the house.

* * * * * *

As we have seen in this chapter, families are systems that function as peoplemakers. Healthy families produce healthy children. In Chapter 10, we will look at disturbed and disorganized families, and the kind of children they produce.

Chapter 10

DISTRESS IN THE SOCIAL SYSTEM

As we have seen, Baby Lyle has been blessed with a family that is both secure and stimulating, and, as a result, he has the needed physical and psychological stamina to take on a variety of roles. Initial roles develop within family boundaries; later ones extend into the neighborhood, school, and community. In Chapter 9, we observed Lyle's mastery of self-help and interpersonal skills. As children attain social milestones, they become not only more sociable, but more socialized.

In this chapter, we will look at sources of stress coming both from within and from outside the family. We will also look at how the nature of some roles may prove stressful for certain children. As before, we will meet four children in this chapter who experience distress to the social system at different points of development.

Children whose primary disturbance is in the social system may receive a variety of educational labels when they are of school age. These may include **mentally retarded, emotionally disturbed, speech and language delayed, and learning disabled.**

Table 10-I
EDUCATIONAL LABELS OF CHILDREN WHOSE PRIMARY DISTRESS
IS TO THE SOCIAL SYSTEM

| Mentally Retarded |
| Emotionally Disturbed |
| Speech and Language Delayed |
| Learning Disabled |

DISTRESS – BIRTH THROUGH INFANCY

At birth, the family system engulfs Baby and draws it into its midst. Time together following birth permits mother, father, and

153

baby to meld together into a family unit. At first this unit consists of mother plus baby and father. As Baby becomes a more active participant, he or she separates from mother, merges with the baby role, and generates expectations for other family members.

The addition of a baby to a family changes the way the primary members relate to one another. To the roles of husband and wife are added new role requirements of father and mother. In healthy families, adjustments are made and bonding is achieved. This natural process of becoming a family can be disrupted because of the influence of a number of factors. These factors differ widely in their degree of severity, and, therefore, their impact upon the family. They include early life in an institution, serial foster homes, separations from home, children with problems, and troubled families.

Early Life in an Institution

One can hardly imagine a situation any worse than for a baby to come into the world and discover that no family awaits. Mothers who relinquish their babies to the state presumably do so because they are unable to provide the necessary physical and/or emotional care. Many relinquished children are adopted right away and so do not suffer the effects of institutional life. Problems occur for those whose stay is indefinite.

In a now classic study, Spitz (1965) studied a group of infants receiving institutional care. Because of the great demands upon the nurses' time, Spitz determined that each infant received, at best, time which would be equal to "one tenth of a mother." While physical care of the babies was adequate, there was little person-to-person contact between nurses and babies and very little stimulation of any kind. Bottles were laid beside babies in their cribs during feeding time. To keep the infants quiet at other times, blankets were hung over the foot and side railings of the beds, screening babies from all visual input except a view of the ceiling.

By the end of the first year, thirty percent of the babies had died; an additional eight percent died during the second year. These infants experienced not only the loss of mother, but loss of family. When a mother is lost to her baby because of death, ill health, desertion, or other reasons, another family member can take on the mother role. In institutional settings, no one is available to adequately fulfill the mothering needs of each individual baby.

Serial Foster Homes

While foster home placement itself need not be traumatic for a child, placement in one foster home after another can have devastating effects on a child's emotional and social development. If an infant does not have a consistent home for the first year of life, there will be no opportunity for the baby to attach to a mother figure. Abrupt moves from one home to another can rupture bonding that may have begun.

Separations from Home

Some children endure extended separations from home during their infancy, usually because of a physical disability which requires hospital treatment. The effects of the separation depend upon the number and length of hospital stays and whether or not the mother is permitted to stay at the hospital with her baby.

For example, a child born with a cleft palate will require early hospitalization for primary and, later, secondary surgical procedures. This absence from home can interrupt the family bonding process and serve to separate the child from high levels of input available in the home environment. The effect can be delays in the child's acquisition of language and motor milestones.

Children with Problems

As a rule, children who have physical or psychological problems require an inordinate amount of a family's time, energy, and money. For example, a child born with a hearing impairment may need to see both an otologist and audiologist on a regular basis, and may require language therapy, a special school, and added time from Mother at home to stimulate language development.

As another example, the irregular habits of a schizophrenic child may upset the balance of an entire family. A child who does not sleep till dawn, who is easily provoked into a tantrum, and who cannot be comforted when hurt, proves a source of stress for all family members. Because of anticipated disruptions, the family may avoid social outings, thereby cutting off potential sources of support.

A blind baby can be particularly disturbing to a family system. Parents who have dealt with the initial shock of their child's blindness and accepted the disability, will find yet another hurdle to overcome at home—a baby with an alien means of communication. Fraiberg (1974) studied blind infants and their mothers and found that not only do blind babies fail to make eye contact, they do not smile in response to a human face, they do not smile as frequently as do sighted babies, and they smile in a muted way. Fraiberg discovered that these behaviors have a negative value of "not friendly" for family members. As she explains, "What we miss in the blind baby, apart from the eyes that do not see, is the vocabulary of signs and signals that provide the most elementary and vital sense of discourse long before words have meaning" (p. 217).

Troubled Families

Remember, Satir (1972) referred to families as "peoplemakers." Children, who are outputs from a family system, reveal a great deal about the internal workings of the family itself.

The troubled families that Satir has worked with in her role as a family therapist have a number of variables in common. She observed that in such families "self-worth was low; communication was indirect, vague, and not really honest; rules were rigid, inhuman, nonnegotiable, and everlasting; and the linking to society was fearful, placating, and blaming" (p. 4).

Beavers (1972) describes three basic family positions which fall along a continuum-of-functioning from disturbed to healthy. They range from **severely disturbed families** (defined as those who produce an adolescent schizophrenic child) to **mid-range families** (who produce neurotic or behavior-disordered children) to **healthy families** (who show no evidence of children with psychological pathology).

In working with families, Beavers found the atmosphere in

severely disturbed families to be one of hostility, cynicism, hopelessness, and despair. Relationships are unclear and there is maximum fusion among mother, father, and child. A child's autonomy is never encouraged, and, in fact, may be implicitly forbidden. As Beavers explains: "The members of these disturbed families behave as if human closeness is found by thinking and feeling just like another; therefore, individuation is tantamount to rejection and exclusion. Their children grow up haunted by the impossibility of obtaining two goals made incompatible in such a system — the goal of being an individual and the goal of acceptance and companionship" (p. 6).

In mid-range families, Beavers found the atmosphere to be dominated by negative moods of sadness and depression and by criticism of other family members. While mid-range families did allow their children to develop coherent identities, the children were found to have a "modest repertoire of interpersonal skills and a constricted, generally guilt-laden self-image" (p. 16–17).

The farther away families moved from health along the continuum, the more impermeable their psychological and social boundaries became. Individual family members became progressively more closed to each other; they did not talk openly about themselves and did not listen as others talked. Family boundaries were closed off as well. Members rarely ventured outside family boundaries and did not seek energy sources outside the family, such as work, friends, and recreation.

DISTRESS – BIRTH THROUGH INFANCY: BENJAMIN

Erin and Ben Farmer were ready to have their second child. Ben was about to graduate from law school and already had a position lined up for himself at an established law firm in town. As a result, Erin could finally quit her secretarial job and tend full-time to her family. Their daughter, Katie, was four.

The week of Ben's graduation, Erin noted a light rash on her arms. She dismissed it as nerves—her excitement over Ben's graduation. It would be months later before she connected the rash with the little boy in Katie's preschool class who had measles. A month after Ben's graduation, Erin's gynecologist confirmed that she was two months pregnant—a little further along than she had thought.

Erin was almost blissfully happy throughout her pregnancy. For the first time in over five years, she was not working and she was enjoying the time at home to cook real meals for a change and to spend lots of time with Katie. Erin was sorry she had missed out on so much of the day-to-day excitement of Katie's early years and vowed not to do so with the new baby. Ben's job seemed secure, and there was no reason why she would have to return to work unless she chose to.

Erin and Ben began attending prepared childbirth classes. Because her first pregnancy and delivery had gone well, Erin wanted a home birth this time. Ben, however, did not feel comfortable with the idea, so Erin agreed to a hospital delivery.

Erin was surprised by the dreams she had during this pregnancy. She awakened with a start several nights, able to recall only impressions of danger. Her dreams contrasted sharply with the pleasant routine of her day, and she put them out of her mind.

Fortunately, Ben was home from work early the Friday evening Erin went into labor. On the way to the hospital, they dropped Katie off at her grandparents' house.

Labor seemed more intense than the first time, and Erin felt that this baby did not want to come out. She was exhausted when she heard the doctor announce that it was a boy, and she fell asleep.

Hours later, when Erin awakened, Ben was there by her bed holding her hand. He looked exhausted and apparently had not slept. Erin herself had slept fitfully, not wanting to sleep, yet not wanting to awaken either. Ben knew he had to tell her right away, so he blundered ahead, "Our baby Benjamin is blind, but otherwise he is healthy and strong. You may have had measles and didn't know it." Erin remembered the rash. Although she felt numb with shock, she wanted her baby. "I have to see our baby," she pleaded, "even if he can't see me."

DISTRESS IN THE PRESCHOOL YEARS

During their preschool years, most children have their first extended contacts with people outside the family system. By this age, children are toilet trained, are taking increased responsibility for their own physical care, and can play simple games and take turns.

Child behaviors which are the norm within one family-cultural system may be viewed as deviant within another system. For this reason, potential problems are often first identified by teachers when children initially enter preschool or day care centers.

Family variables which place special demands upon a child's ability to cope are single-parent families, blended families, child abuse, poverty, social problems, and overprotective families.

Single-Parent Families

Homes containing only one parent were once referred to as broken homes. Now that such homes may be the rule, rather than the exception, they are not automatically considered to be the reason for a child's learning or behavior problems.

A single-parent family consists of one parent (mother or father), plus one or more natural or adopted children. The majority of such families are headed by mothers and have problems unique to this type of family system.

Hetherington, Cox, and Cox (1979) describe the primary stressors in such families. The first they call "task overload." This occurs when one adult is responsible for the primary financial support of the family, for household maintenance, and for linking the family with the community by way of piano lessons, scouts, PTA etc. The second major problem experienced by mother-headed families is financial duress. Even though child support may have been awarded by a court, many women do not actually receive it, often because their ex-husbands are committed to supporting a second family. A third major problem is social isolation. There may be little family time or money available for friends, church, and community activities. This places Mother in the very uncomfortable position of experiencing added pressures at the same time that she is losing emotional and social support.

Blended Families

Blended families include step, adopted, and/or foster children. Each type of blended family has its own special set of problems.

When two families blend into a step-family, the number of individuals each family member must relate to increases dramatically. For example, when an only child's parents divorce and remarry, the child now must relate to a step-father, a step-mother, and perhaps two sets of step-brothers and sisters. Conflicting allegiances are a major problem for a child in a step-family. He or she now has two of everything—two families, two homes, sometimes two sets of clothes and toys.

Parents who adopt usually cannot have children of their own. Some parents, however, do have their own children and adopt still others. Families who choose to adopt face the stresses of the adoption process, which consists of endless paperwork and delays. Regulations have relaxed somewhat in recent years, so that single parents and homosexual couples may adopt in some states. Such family units have special adjustments to make, as do families who adopt interracial, handicapped, or older children.

Foster families usually function as temporary families for children who must be taken from their natural parents because of a family crisis. Since foster families are, by nature, temporary, it is important for children placed in them to maintain contact with their natural parents to facilitate their eventual return to their homes.

Child Abuse

Child abuse refers to the inflicting of deliberate injuries to a child, usually by a parent. Children who are physically handicapped, mentally retarded, or of difficult temperament are at greatest risk for abuse, because they can produce strain within a vulnerable family, thus precipitating an outbreak of violence. The most common abuses to children are burns, broken bones, bruises, and head injuries. Gelles (1982) reviewed the literature on child abuse and reports that the possibility of child abuse increases when (1) parents themselves were abused as children, (2) the family is of low socioeconomic status, (3) there is unemployment or financial problems within the family or it is a single-parent unit, and (4) the family is socially isolated.

Poverty

There are many risks for a child born into a family that is poor. For one, the family may not have the financial resources available to meet the baby's physical needs for food, shelter, clothing, and medical care.

Life in very poor homes centers around survival. The home itself is often dirty, rundown, and cluttered, not because people who are poor like living this way, but because they lack the financial resources to live otherwise. Appliances such as washing machines, microwave ovens, and frost-free refrigerators, which help make life run smoothly in middle-class homes, are beyond the means of those without charge cards and savings accounts.

Life in poor homes is often disorganized, lacking a routine. There may be no regular meal times, and, from the time they are old enough to tear open a cellophane wrapper, children fend for themselves by downing packaged foods—potato chips and cookies. Thankfully, starvation is rare in the United States, but it is quite common for children from poor families to have substandard nutrition. Children who have eaten no breakfast, or, perhaps even worse, have had a donut and coke, may be sluggish or hard to arouse. Such children's curiosity about the world is dulled.

Oscar Lewis (1959), an anthropologist who popularized the term "culture of poverty" explains: "Poverty becomes a dynamic factor which affects participation in the larger national cultures and creates a subculture of its own. One can speak of the culture of the poor, for it has its own modalities and distinctive social and psychological consequences for its members" (p. 2).

Sarbin (1970) delineates three characteristics of the culture of poverty: (1) "an exclusive time orientation to the present," (2) linguistic patterns which "reflect the monotony of sensory inputs" available in poor environments, and (3) a belief in fate and luck which typify the poor's convictions that "events are controlled by external forces" (pp. 32–35).

Such ways of believing catch individual members in a web of self-limiting perceptions. The problem is not only that the poor are unable to pull free from this entrapment, but that they do not even know they are caught.

Social Problems

Problems such as alcoholism and drug abuse serve to disorganize families, break down communication, and, in some cases, elicit violence. Alcohol or drug abuse can interfere with a mother's or father's ability to be emotionally available to their children and to care for them financially. Adults who habitually have hangovers are unreliable, or perhaps explosive, and are unable to provide a stable support system for growing children.

Overprotective Families

Here we refer to families who shelter a child from the social demands of the family and community. Children may be overly protected because of a physical or psychological disability, or because they are shy by temperament. Overprotected children usually are late in developing self-care and interpersonal skills; they are ill at ease in social situations and may have difficulty adapting to the demands of school.

DISTRESS – PRESCHOOL YEARS: SHAMETRA

Shametra was a tiny, small-for-dates baby born to Shirley Curd, a black teenager not quite 16. Shirley lived with her mother and seven brothers and sisters in an old, rundown house in an all-black area of a small town. Her two older sisters also had babies, so Shirley and her baby brought the total number of occupants of their three-bedroom house to twelve.

Following her sisters' example, Shirley signed up for aid-to-dependent-children benefits as soon as possible after Shametra was born. Shirley had dropped out of school and was too young to work; it fell to her to stay home and babysit while her sisters went to their jobs at the box factory where their mother also worked.

The three babies, all under the age of two, never seemed to stop crying, and Shametra seemed the most irritable. Shirley did not like breastfeeding, and so she switched to the formula her sisters used. Sometimes she would put all the babies in one bedroom and close the door so she would not have to hear their screaming; then she would watch television or play her brother's tape player with the headphones on. When her younger sisters came in from school, Shirley could usually persuade one of them to watch the babies while she went to the store for groceries.

When her older sisters came home from work, they eagerly fetched their babies and spent the evening in play with them. By evening, Shirley was tired of babies, and she usually let Shametra lie in her crib. The baby was so tiny that other family members seemed hesitant to pick her up; "cause she might break," Shirley's brother said.

When Shametra was two, Shirley took a job at the same factory where her sisters and mother worked. All three sisters left their babies at a day care center. Shametra was still very small for her age and not yet toilet trained.

The director of the day care center was used to poverty children; however, she was a bit surprised by Shametra's appearance. Her clothes were not just old, they were dirty. And the diaper bag that accompanied Shametra to the center contained a change of other worn-out clothes, a sack of crumbled cookies, and a baby bottle full of soda pop.

The director observed Shametra for the first week. She noted that the little girl was withdrawn and did not join in play with the other children. At lunch she picked at her food with her fingers, eating little. Shametra could be coaxed into taking a nap only when given her bottle of pop. She would suck on the bottle and twist her hair with her fingers until she fell asleep. When the director became convinced that no improvement was likely, she called the department of public welfare and asked to talk with Shirley's caseworker.

DISTRESS IN THE SCHOOL YEARS

Children who experience distress in the school years either do not have the physical or psychological stamina required to assume the role of student, or they find the role to be at odds with their role experiences within their family and cultural group.

The increased emphasis on mastery and competence in the school years proves especially stressful for children with physical disabilities or emotional instability and those with either learning patterns or lifestyles which fail to mesh with classroom requirements.

During the school years, children's drawings of their families are excellent indicators of the tenor of family life. Their portrayal of individual expressions, interactions among family members, and the child's perception of his or her importance within the family are all noteworthy.

Some socio-cultural factors which influence the functioning of a child in the school years are: high levels of stress, diet, school readiness, learning style, and low socioeconomic status.

High Levels of Stress

David Elkind, author of **The Hurried Child** (1981), describes ways in which children are hastened into adulthood. Even first-grade children seem to be miniature adults. They wear designer jeans, travel alone by plane, take part in highly competitive sports, and are required to bring home A's on their first report card.

Latch-key children are another phenomenon of our society. They are so-called because they carry their own key to their homes and let themselves in after school. During the two or more hours before their parents come home from work, many latch-key children are required to do household chores and complete their homework, and sometimes even prepare dinner.

Type A behavior, once thought to be characteristic of long-term competition among adults, is now being uncovered in some children. Elkind (1981) explains: "Type A behavior (high-strung, competitive, demanding) has been identified in children and associated with heightened cholesterol levels. It has also been associated with parental pressure for achievement" (p. 14).

Elkind defines stressors as events that are not necessarily bad or good but, rather, are just "special demands." Too many special demands in a given period of time will eventually precipitate a change in the child's health and/or behavior. Examples of life events which may prove stressful range from the obviously traumatic (death of a parent, divorce, birth of a sibling) to the more benign (vacation with family, attending summer camp, going to a birthday party).

It is important to mention here a special group of children, referred to by psychologists as **invulnerables.** These may be offspring of alcoholic parents or schizophrenic mothers, or they may be children who are abused or extremely poor. The dimension all invulnerables share is their emotional strength. Given a family situation that would produce a breakdown in most children, they "respond to stress by developing extraordinary competence" (Pines, 1979, p. 53).

Diet

While food intake primarily affects the biological system, what one chooses to eat is a product of family and culture. As we have noted, children from poor families often have marginal diets which inhibit their readiness for learning. Middle-class children have their own problems in relation to diet. Many are overfed on nutritionally-poor diets (presweetened cereals, soft drinks, potato chips, candy bars), producing what Brody (1981) calls the "junk food generation."

Certain children may be sensitive to the artificial colors, flavors, and preservatives used in abundance in packaged and processed foods. The symptoms of these sensitivities include sleeplessness, hyperactivity, and aggression (Feingold, 1979). Allergies to common foods such as milk, eggs, fish, wheat, and corn may cause headaches, nausea, hyperactivity, and fatigue (Springer, 1982). When a diet-related problem results in overactivity and inattentiveness, a child's school performance is affected.

School Readiness

The term **school readiness** was coined by the staff of the Gesell Institute for Human Development. They observed that many children start school before they are physically mature enough to handle the demands of a classroom setting. As a rule, boys' development in the early years is slower than that of girls'. A boy whose chronological age is six may have a behavior age of five-and-a-half, indicating that kindergarten would be a more appropriate placement for him than would first-grade.

The Gesell Institute has developed a battery of tests, the Developmental Placement Tests, for use in determining accurate school placement (Ilg, Ames, Haines, and Gillespie, 1978). Children who begin school before they are physically ready are referred to as "overplaced" (Ames, 1978). Overplacement signs include undue fatigue, stomachaches in the morning before school, trouble sleeping or crankiness, and choosing friends from a lower grade level.

Learning Style

The major tasks of first grade are learning to read, spell, and work arithmetic problems. Children with the learning style of **listener/looker** seem to make the easiest adjustment to early learning demands. For these children, both auditory and visual channels are readied, and auditory and visual memory are adequate to the tasks at hand. They can easily sound out words, recall sight words, read aloud, spell, and print legibly.

Children who are **listeners** or **lookers** tend to have more difficulty with first-grade work. Just how much difficulty they experience will depend upon how early their struggles are detected and whether or not support services are available.

The child with a **mover** style probably experiences the most difficulty of all. Children whose orientation to learning is through movement and touch no doubt will feel trapped at their desks. They will be stifled by rules of staying in line, speaking softly, and reading silently. They may find the only places they can be themselves are in the lunch room and on the playground.

Low Socioeconomic Status

For many children from lower socioeconomic homes, their first collision with middle-class norms and values comes when they enter the public schools. These children do not easily fit into the role of student. Faced with classroom norms of cleanliness, quietness, and obedience, poor children may withdraw within and expose little of themselves in the student role.

Children born into the culture of poverty probably do not know how to play soccer; they are not familiar with fairy tales; and they may never have had a book of their own. This is not to say that they have not had valuable experiences in their early years, but, rather, that many of these experiences have been different from those of middle-class children. Such children may pull back as a means of protection from the unknown, and they may be labeled by their teachers (who do not understand the dynamics of roles) as shy, withdrawn, or even, perhaps, uncooperative.

Deutsch (1967) points out: "We know that it is difficult for all peoples to span cultural discontinuities, and yet we make little if any effort to prepare administrative personnel or teachers and guidance staff to assist the child in this transition from one cultural context to another" (p. 40). Anastasiow, Hanes, and Hanes (1982) explain: "Middle-class children come to school achievement-oriented, future-directed, and encouraged to develop their own talents and individuality. Lower-class children come to school oriented toward the present, loyal to their friends and family, and anxious to be accepted by their peers and neighbors. The first set of values has been productive in having children succeed in school, the other has not" (p. 110).

No doubt children experience even more difficulty in assuming the student role if they are of a differing ethnic group—Black, Hispanic, or Indian—from their classmates. Children who speak a separate language or a dialect of English are confronted with yet another barrier to communication with their teachers and classmates.

Oakland (1977) critiques standardized testing as it relates to minority groups. The tests themselves are biased and unfair to persons from cultural and socioeconomic minorities, because they reflect largely white, middle-class values and attitudes. Further, the tests are oftentimes conducted by professionals who do not understand the home culture and language of a particular minority group. Finally, test scores set up expectations for teachers. They tend to expect poor performance from children who score low on tests of intellectual functioning. Such expectations function as **self-fulfilling prophecies,** a topic discussed in Chapter 2.

Figure 10-1. Points of possible distress to the developing social system.

Following are profiles of two children who represent two very different types of distress to the social system.

DISTRESS—THE SCHOOL YEARS: JAKE

Almost every night Jake was awakened sometime after midnight by his parents' fighting. Usually, his father had just come in from the 3-to-11 shift at the factory, after having stopped off for a few drinks on his way home. One morning Jake awoke to find an overturned bookcase in the living room and books strewn all about. That afternoon when Jake came home from school, Laura, his mother, was waiting for him with their bags packed. The apartment they moved to was tiny; Jake slept on the sofa in the living room.

Within a few months, Laura had obtained a divorce. Shortly after, she began dating a man at work. On Friday and Saturday nights, Jake would stay with his grandmother, returning home Sunday morning. Soon, Laura was talking about marrying Ed. She asked Jake if he was ready to have a new father. All Jake knew was that he hadn't seen his own father in months, and he missed him.

Whether Jake was ready or not, the wedding date was set. Laura and Ed had a small church ceremony. Ed's two children were there—a boy, nine, and a girl, eight, who lived with their mother in a nearby city.

Jake had just settled into Ed's house, when his mother announced more news. Ed had taken a sales job in the city where his ex-wife and children lived. Ed's son wanted to live with his father, so Jake would be sharing a room with his step-brother. His step-sister would visit every other weekend.

Jake was spinning from all the changes. He actually felt dizzy when he woke up some mornings. At the end of the summer, he was enrolled by his mother in a third-grade class in his new school. Jake, who was used to riding his bike to school, now had to go to school by bus.

Jake's stomach was churning the first morning of school. He couldn't remember ever before being scared about going to school. All the faces around him were strange, and he felt as if everyone was staring at him. Jake was self-conscious because he didn't have new clothes for school as he had at the start of other school years. Laura had been short of money because of the move, and his dad was in a hospital to "dry out" and couldn't afford to help.

Jake's stomach hurt after lunch every day that first week of school. His teacher became concerned and sent him to the school nurse. She called his mother at work and asked her to come pick him up. Jake felt scared as he waited for her on the front steps of the school. He knew she would be mad at him for bothering her the first week at her new job.

DISTRESS – THE SCHOOL YEARS: RYAN

Ryan Begay spent the first six years of his life on a Navajo reservation in New Mexico. His parents had grown up there, too, as had his grandparents and great-grandparents. Ryan wore his hair long and straight, as did his cousin, Betty. She dressed in typical tribal attire for little girls, gathered skirt and a velvet blouse. Ryan wore a western shirt, tennis shoes, and jeans.

Ryan's father, James, had recently begun to talk about leaving the reservation, because there was little work, and he was not willing to draw unemployment. Both Ryan's and Betty's parents made plans to move to a small town near the reservation. One afternoon, the brothers caught a ride into town. They applied for jobs on the construction crew of the new post office building going up there, and were both hired. The two families packed their few possessions for the move. Neither family had a car, so they moved into a small rented house in town close enough for the men to walk to work. While the house was small for six people, it had a bathroom and running water, neither of which had been available in their living quarters on the reservation.

Since the children's fathers had good jobs, there was money for new clothes for school. In the department store, Ryan felt the clerk's eyes on him as he removed his worn-out tennis shoes and tried on a brand-new pair. He also got a new pair of jeans and a t-shirt with a picture of "E.T." on the front. He laughed when he saw Betty in her first pair of knickers.

Next stop was a barber shop. Ryan watched as the barber swept away a pile of his hair. He refused to look at himself in the mirror, and he did not dare tell his mother of his sadness at losing his hair.

The first day of school, their mothers walked them to the school yard and shooed them into their classrooms. Ryan and Betty were in separate first-grade classes. Ryan hated to leave his cousin. He could count on her to talk for him when he didn't feel up to it.

A teacher greeted Ryan. She bent down, looked him in the eye, and asked him his name. He told her quickly and then looked away. He was the only Indian child in the class.

A week of school passed and Ryan still had not spoken aloud in class. Other than hearing him say his name on the first day of school, Mrs. Clendon had not heard him speak. When she tried to catch his eye or call on him in class, he would look away, hanging his head. On the playground, he and Betty huddled together watching the children's games and refusing to join in. When the speech-language pathologist came to her room asking for referrals of children with communication problems, Mrs. Clendon suggested that Ryan be tested.

* * * * * *

In Chapter 11, we will follow Benjamin, Shametra, Jake, and Ryan from the first recognition of their social system distress through evaluation and treatment. We will take special note of how their ability to relate to others has been impaired.

Chapter 11

PROMOTING WELLBEING
AT THE SOCIAL LEVEL

From the outset, we know that the major disturbance of the children in this chapter is in the social system. The initial signs of their disturbance may express as lags in biological, psychological, or social development, or a combination of these three. Recall that social milestones are reflected in interactions with others and in the attainment of self-help skills which foster independence.

In the development of Benjamin, Shametra, Jake, and Ryan, we will observe social system disturbances as evidenced by one or more of the following:

- Disturbance in relationships with family members.
- Inability to fulfill role requirements at school or with peers.
- Lag in self-help skills.

Disturbances in the social system may be coupled with:

- Delays in language and/or motor milestones (biological system).
- Disturbance in emotional development or self-concept (psychological system).
- A case history event which suggests distress in the social system (See History of a Child's Social System, Table 11-II).

Each of the children we will be following evidences a different variation of the above patterns. Two have developmental delays in one system only, one in two systems, and another in all three systems.

172

Table 11-I

DEVELOPMENTAL PATTERNS WHICH SIGNAL A POSSIBLE DISTURBANCE
TO THE SOCIAL SYSTEM

• Disturbance in relationships with family members

• Inability to fulfill role requirements at school or with peers

• Lag in self-help skills

• Delays in language and/or motor milestones (biological system)

• Disturbance in emotional development or self-concept (psychological system)

• A case history event which suggests distress in the social system

Table 11-II

HISTORY OF A CHILD'S SOCIAL SYSTEM

FAMILY MAKEUP
    Is the family intact?
    Is this a single parent family?
        Blended family? If so, step? adopted? foster?
    How many other children in the home?
    Does anyone else live with the family?
    Socioeconomic status of family?
    Ethnic group?
    What is the language of the home?
    What kind of work outside the home do mother and father do?

PHYSICAL ENVIRONMENT OF HOME
    Describe the physical conditions of home (if home visit has been made).
    Any indicators of an understimulating or overstimulating environment?
    Does family have regular meals? Describe their eating habits.

PARENT-CHILD RELATIONSHIPS
    Does the father take part in child care?
    How do mother-father-child interact?
    What is family life like; is there a routine?

SCHOOL
    Has child been to preschool? Any problems?
    Has child been to school? Any problems?
    How are child's relationships with peers?

COMMUNITY
    Does family take part in community activities?
        Church? Neighborhood? School?

BENJAMIN

Ben was worried about his wife. She seemed determined to act as if nothing were wrong with their baby. When a couple from a local association for the blind called, offering to come by and share their experiences about their own blind son, Erin politely refused. Later, she explained to Ben that they were doing fine, so there was nothing to discuss.

Outwardly, Erin appeared cheerful nearly all the time, but Ben felt that there must be a lot of sadness behind her smiles. He, himself, had shed many tears since his son's birth, usually when he was alone in the car. He had tried to tell Erin about these times, but she refused to make time to talk with him.

Ben found relating to his son to be somewhat puzzling. He missed the eye-to-eye contact he had so enjoyed with Katie. And, this baby smiled so little. When Ben picked up Benjamin from his crib, the anticipated smile was not there. Both sets of grandparents seemed sensitive to this lack of feedback, and Ben noted that they did not come as often as they had. By two months of age, Benjamin was grasping a rattle placed in his hand, but no squeals or laughter accompanied his play.

One evening after dinner, when both children were asleep and Erin was unusually tired from her day, she started crying and could not stop. "Benjamin must know it's my fault he's blind. He won't respond to me because he can't forgive me." Ben reassured her that it was not just Erin's problem, but that the whole family needed help in dealing with Benjamin. Finally, Erin agreed to a meeting with the Brandons, the couple who had called a month before.

The Brandons were about the same age as the Farmers. He was an accountant; his wife, a teacher. Their blind son was their second child, and they had had a third child since. The Brandons were open in describing their shock, hurt, and anger following the birth of their son. Erin was most interested to hear of the difficulty they had had in relating to their blind baby. The Brandons described him as unfriendly and aloof. Through the parent group, they had learned that these behaviors are typical of all blind babies, who relate differently than sighted ones. Slowly, they had

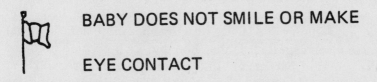

BABY DOES NOT SMILE OR MAKE

EYE CONTACT

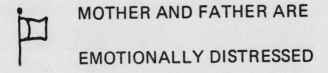

MOTHER AND FATHER ARE

EMOTIONALLY DISTRESSED

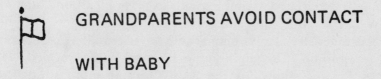

GRANDPARENTS AVOID CONTACT

WITH BABY

Figure 11-1. Red flags signaling the need for Benjamin's family to seek an evaluation.

learned to adapt themselves to their son.

Ben and Erin talked for hours after the Brandons left. Erin wanted to know more about blindness. She and Ben agreed to take Benjamin, now three months old, to a psychologist at the League for the Blind for developmental evaluation.

The psychologist tested Benjamin using the **Denver Developmental Screening Test,** modified a bit to account for differences in the development of blind children. Benjamin's development proved to be at age level in most areas and slightly above in others.

In observing mother-child interactions, the psychologist noted that Erin was primarily visual in her approach to her baby. When asked about her favored style of learning, Erin acknowledged that she, in fact, was a visual learner. She remembered learning to read by sight as a child; she had operated a computer in her work; and her hobby was art. The psychologist suggested that she become more aware of the ways she initiated contact with her baby, and that she add auditory and tactile stimuli to her more natural visual mode. He also suggested: 1) that Ben and Erin become involved with the group of parents of blind children that met regularly at the League for the Blind facility, and 2) mobility training for Benjamin as soon as he began to crawl. Erin would be shown ways to encourage Benjamin to explore his environment, while offering him maximum protection.

With practice, Erin became more and more attuned to her baby's learning style. She bought musical toys for his room, and at the end of his crib she put a busy-box of objects to turn, pull, and feel. Ben put wheels on the baby's crib so that Erin could push him from room to room as she worked during the day. She brought Benjamin in the kitchen each evening so he could take in the sounds and smells of food being prepared. During her daily work routine, Erin talked to him, describing what was going on around him.

By five months, Benjamin was running his fingers over his parents' and sister's faces. A faint smile would cross his lips, indicating recognition. "Benjamin knows it's me," Katie squealed, "He knows I'm his sister." As the family became more attuned to Benjamin's special needs, he became more responsive to them.

Table 11-III
SUMMARY OF BENJAMIN'S EVALUATION AND TREATMENT PLAN

Primary System Disturbance:	Social
Template/Environment:	Normal-to-superior range of intelligence
	Needs more auditory and tactile stimulation
Learning Style:	Listener/mover
Treatment Plan:	Social system—parent support group; mobility training

SHAMETRA

It was a bright, sunlit day when Mrs. Burns, the child welfare worker, knocked at the front door of the Curd home. Shirley let her into a house that was dismally dark inside. Some of the windows were covered with old velvet curtains; the others were so dirty it was impossible to see out. Shirley and Shametra were sitting in the dark in front of a small black-and-white television set. The living room was strewn with toys, clothes, and beer cans. There were dishes with dried food on them stacked on the end tables.

Mrs. Burns discovered that Shirley had been laid off from her job and was now spending her days at home with Shametra. Mrs. Burns asked about Shametra's birth. Shirley brought out the birth certificate, and Mrs. Burns noted that the baby was very small for full-term, only four pounds. Shirley was unable to give the dates of any developmental milestones.

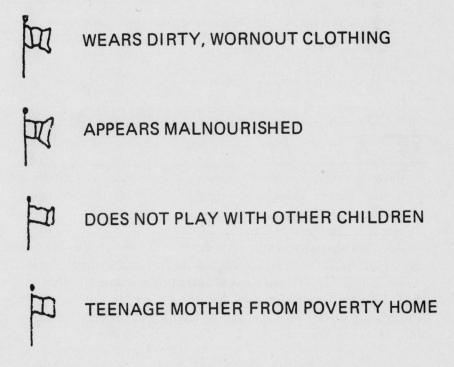

WEARS DIRTY, WORNOUT CLOTHING

APPEARS MALNOURISHED

DOES NOT PLAY WITH OTHER CHILDREN

TEENAGE MOTHER FROM POVERTY HOME

Figure 11-2. The day care director's observations of Shametra which point to a disturbance in the social system.

Shametra peered from behind the sofa at the visitor. When she was convinced there was no danger, she scurried out to retrieve a toy. Mrs. Burns tried to engage the little girl in conversation. Shametra brought her baby doll in. "Baby doll," she said, "My baby."

Mrs. Burns estimated the child's intellectual abilities to be at least in the low average range, perhaps higher. She did not appear as delayed as one might expect considering her inadequate diet and insufficient stimulation.

The child welfare worker told Shirley about a class for young mothers at the neighborhood health care center. There she could meet girls her own age and learn some new things about caring for her child. Babysitting was provided, and Mrs. Burns would pick her up and take her each week. Eager for a way to get out of the house, Shirley agreed to go.

For Shirley, going to the neighborhood center each week was like going to a party. There were talks and films on child care and nutrition, and time afterward to talk with the other girls, many of whom Shirley had known in junior high school. Most, like Shirley, still lived at home and had one or more babies to care for.

Shirley observed how the other girls played with their babies and how they dressed them. She wanted Shametra to look as cute as the other children, but since she wasn't working she didn't have money to buy clothes. Mrs. Burns arranged to take her to a child-clothing co-op, where Shirley could get used children's clothing for a small charge. She also arranged for the nutritionist from the health center to make a home visit and talk with Shirley about inexpensive, but nutritious, meals and snacks.

Mrs. Burns continued to provide support services to Shirley and Shametra for over two years. At the end of that time, Shirley moved out of her mother's house and into an apartment that she and Shametra would share with another young mother (and her child) who Shirley had met at the health center. While Shirley continued to receive welfare payments, she was ready to do some work outside the home. She took a part-time job washing dishes in a neighborhood restaurant and planned to go to work full-time when Shametra started to school.

Table 11-IV
SUMMARY OF SHAMETRA'S EVALUATION AND TREATMENT PLAN

Primary System Disturbance:	Social
Template/Environment:	Estimated to be low average to average range of intelligence
	Inadequate stimulation in all channels
Learning Style:	Not yet known
Treatment Plan:	Social system—health education services from child welfare worker; weekly sessions at neighborhood health center
	Biological system—nutritional consultation

JAKE

As soon as Jake and his mother reached home, he ran into the bathroom and threw up. Laura was waiting for him when he emerged from the bathroom, pale and shaken. She told him to lie down, and she put a wet towel over his forehead. "I've got to talk to your teacher, Jake, and find out what's wrong."

Laura was surprised to learn from Jake's teacher what a hard time her son was having adjusting to school. He had been well-liked at his old school, had excelled in sports, and was a good student. Now he was withdrawn and rarely turned in his assignments. The teacher suggested testing by the school psychometrist to pinpoint the nature of Jake's learning problems, and Laura readily agreed to this plan.

In the conference following the testing, Laura learned that Jake had no learning disabilities to explain his learning problems. His test scores were in the superior range on both the Verbal and Performance scales of the WISC–R. Jake's drawing of his family, however, revealed his perception of the threatening nature of family life. The psychometrist asked if during the past year there had been other changes besides the move in Jake's life.

Laura related a string of events, beginning with her separation and, later, her divorce from Jake's father. Her remarriage occurred soon after, followed by a move to a new house in a new town, a new family, school, teacher, and classmates. Laura was stunned as she counted the number of changes Jake had experienced. It was the

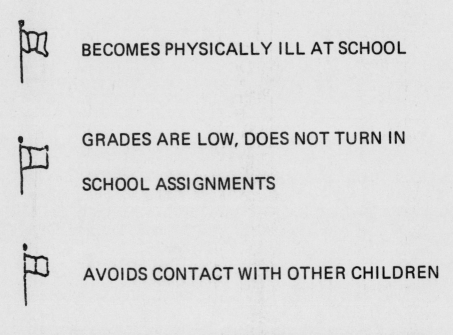

BECOMES PHYSICALLY ILL AT SCHOOL

GRADES ARE LOW, DOES NOT TURN IN

SCHOOL ASSIGNMENTS

AVOIDS CONTACT WITH OTHER CHILDREN

Figure 11-3. Indicators that Jake is experiencing distress within the social system.

first time she had seen the family situation through his eyes. She realized that she had expected the impossible—the blending of five strangers into an instant happy family.

The psychometrist suggested that Laura talk with the school counselor a few times for help in finding ways to manage and reduce Jake's level of stress. Additionally, he arranged for Jake to see the school counselor weekly.

Jake began to look forward to seeing the counselor each week. There had been so much activity at home that it was always difficult to find the time or place for Jake and his mother to talk. It was great to have someone's undivided attention.

Laura, too, benefited from her visits to the counselor. With his help, she realized that Jake had been forced to sever relationships with family and friends, and, in fact, all the hometown people he

Figure 11-4. Jake's drawing of his family reveals that he perceives family life to be threatening.

had known his eight years of life. Since Jake was old enough to travel short distances by bus, he could spend some weekends with his grandmother, and his father could visit him there.

Jake was uneasy about his first meeting with his father. His dad was sober when he picked Jake up at his grandmother's, and after they had spent a while together, it began to feel like old times — only better, because there was no fighting.

To help Jake make friends, the counselor suggested that his mother sign him up for Boy Scouts or a softball team. Taking part in these activities, Jake became acquainted with the neighborhood boys. Ed accompanied him on Jake's first father-son overnight camping trip.

Finally, Jake needed regular time alone with his mother. Each week, Laura picked Jake up from his Scout meeting and they went out, just the two of them, for a coke. Laura and Ed made a change in one of their plans — they had talked of having a child of their own. Now they put that idea on hold for a couple of years until all the family members had had time to adjust to one another and their new living arrangements.

By the second semester, Jake was making a recovery at school. His grades were nearly up to his old standards, and he had three best friends.

Table 11-V
SUMMARY OF JAKE'S EVALUATION AND TREATMENT PLAN

Primary System Disturbance:	Social system
Template/Environment:	Superior range of intellectual functioning
	Adequate as a baby, Experiencing stimuli overload now
Learning Style:	Listener/looker/mover
Treatment Plan:	Social system—counseling for mother to help her reduce Jake's level of stress; Boy Scouts, softball team; renew contacts with father and grandmother
	Psychological system—individual therapy for Jake

RYAN

Mrs. Neil, a speech-language pathologist, had never tested an Indian child before. To develop rapport with Ryan, she sat in the swing next to his on the playground during recess and introduced herself. She told him she would come to his classroom after lunch and ask him some questions. She asked which playground toy he liked best. "The monkey bars," he answered.

Ryan's eyes were downcast as Mrs. Neil fetched him from his classroom, took his hand, and led him to her room in the school basement. The first test she used was for articulation skills, to measure his ability to produce the sounds of English. She showed Ryan pictures and asked him to say their names out loud, but there was no response from Ryan. "Come on," she encouraged him, "I'm sure you can say monkey and broom."

Mrs. Neil moved on to the vocabulary test. She showed Ryan four pictures and asked him to point to the one she named. This time Ryan complied for awhile and pointed to each word. However, after a sequence of three words that Ryan apparently did not

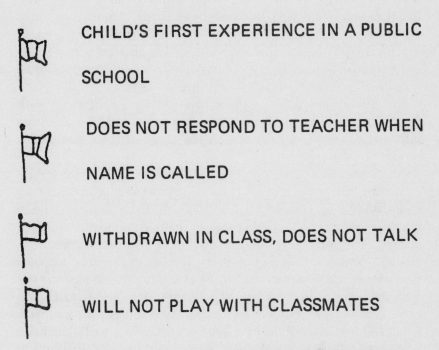

CHILD'S FIRST EXPERIENCE IN A PUBLIC SCHOOL

DOES NOT RESPOND TO TEACHER WHEN NAME IS CALLED

WITHDRAWN IN CLASS, DOES NOT TALK

WILL NOT PLAY WITH CLASSMATES

Figure 11-5. His teacher's concerns about Ryan's social development.

know — parachute, capsule, and penguin — he sat back in his seat with his shoulders hunched and refused to point any more.

Mrs. Neil was unable to complete her test battery, and she was not sure if any of her test results could be considered valid anyway. She had heard that a class was being offered in testing minority-group children at the university where she had graduated. Knowing she was in need of consultation, she called the university and asked to speak with the teacher of that class.

The university's education professor told Mrs. Neil that Indian children often do not respond to articulation testing. If they haven't been tested before, they don't know how to play the role of a child being tested. They don't understand why they are being asked to tell the names of pictures that the teacher must already know. Mrs. Neil learned, too, that life in Indian homes is quieter than that of white, middle-class homes. Indian children are not usually encouraged to be verbally expressive. Also, standard measures of intelligence, such as the WISC–R and the Peabody, cannot be counted on to give a reliable estimate of an Indian child's intellectual functioning. The professor urged Mrs. Neil and the school's personnel to concern themselves with easing Ryan's transition into a white world rather than with obtaining test data.

The speech-language pathologist asked for a conference with the principal and with Ryan's classroom teacher. She related the information she had gained, and the three of them outlined a number of steps to be taken.

While the school had a policy that members of the same family could not be in the same classroom, they decided in this case the rule could be broken. Ryan and his cousin Betty needed to be in the same classroom so that neither of them would feel so isolated.

Mrs. Neil volunteered to make a home visit once a month to talk with Ryan's and Betty's mothers. She would explain classroom procedures and expectations for the children's progress. This was a bit different from the kinds of activities Mrs. Neil usually performed in her job, but she welcomed the challenge. In addition, Mrs. Neil would see Ryan and Betty together for a half hour twice a week to talk with them about school customs and to find out about their home on the reservation. In this way, she hoped to encourage them to talk more at school.

As the children grew more comfortable with school, their teacher, Mrs. Clendon, asked if they would bring some mementos of their life on the reservation for show-and-tell. The teacher read the class a story about an Indian brave, and, afterward, Ryan and Betty showed pictures of themselves in native dress. They passed around a turquoise ring, leather moccasins, and a handcrafted basket from the reservation. Next morning, two first-graders stopped by Ryan's and Betty's house and waited to walk to school with them.

* * * * * *

In our final chapter, we will see how the biological, psychological, and social threads of a child's life intertwine.

Table 11-VI
SUMMARY OF RYAN'S EVALUATION AND TREATMENT PLAN

Primary System Disturbance:	Social
Template/Environment:	Probably normal range
	Stimulating, but does not encourage verbal expression
Learning Style:	Looker
Treatment Plan:	Social system—put both children in same classroom; speech-language pathologist acts as liaison between home and school; communication therapy twice weekly to encourage verbal skills

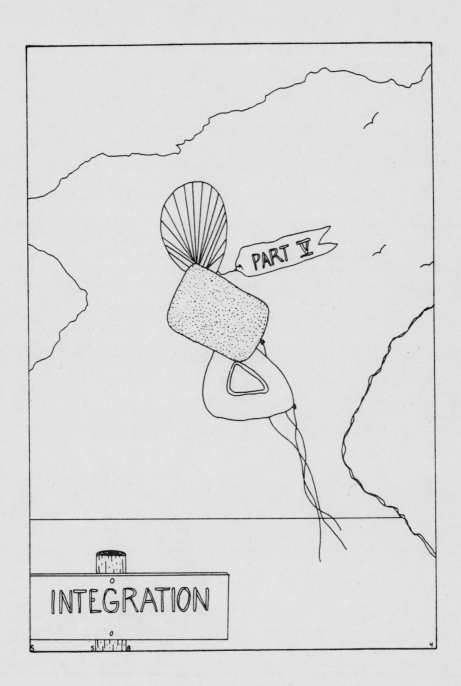

Chapter 12

INTEGRATION

Thus far, we have isolated the biological, psychological, and social systems of a child for in-depth study. Now, in our minds, we must put the hypothetical pieces back together again. The purpose of this chapter is to integrate information from earlier chapters in the areas of systems theory, child development, and evaluation. We begin with a review of terminology used in systems theory.

SYSTEMS THEORY

Open System

To say that a living system is open means that it readily permits inputs of matter, energy, and information to cross its boundaries. The physical body, the mother-child unit, and the family are all open systems. The health of a system depends upon the degree of permeability of its boundary, so to maintain vitality, systems must remain open.

All systems require supplies from their environments in order to survive. The type of supplies depends upon the nature of the system. The physical body demands supplies in the form of food, water, and information. Environmental requirements to nurture the development of personality are caring, holding, and caressing, particularly from Mother. The family is supported by its links to other social systems within the community, such as school, church, and other families.

Inputs

The informational input most critical to the life of a system occurs at conception with the merging of genetic information from mother and father. The genetic template defines a new human being's intellectual limits, sensory capabilities, learning style, and motivation to learn. Genetic defects can be carried by recessive or dominant genes or produced by missing, extra, or abnormal chromosomes. Handicaps which can result include Down Syndrome, inborn errors of metabolism, and cleft palate.

The next series of inputs to the developing child-system occurs within the fetal environment. A mother's diet, as well as her emotional state, affect the physical and emotional wellbeing of the baby growing within her. Lack of optimum nutritional inputs, such as protein or vitamin deficiencies, can hamper the development of the fetus, as can teratogens, such as toxic drugs, radiation, and infections. Some handicaps brought about in the womb are mental retardation, hearing impairment, and cerebral palsy.

During the hazardous journey through the birth canal, problems with the umbilical cord or hemorrhaging by the mother can diminish that most critical of inputs—oxygen. A breech birth or forceps delivery can produce an overload of input to the fetal head. Both lack of oxygen and injury to the head at this critical time can permanently damage a baby's central nervous system, resulting in handicaps such as learning disabilities, mental retardation, and cerebral palsy.

Once the journey from the womb to the outside world is complete, babies become immersed in physical and social stimulation. Three distinct communication bands bear information from environment to baby in the form of sights, sounds, and sensations. Economically-poor homes may provide informational inputs which are insufficient to move a child to the programmed upper limits of his or her abilities. Some families may overload a particularly sensitive baby with too much input; other families may provide mainly one-channel input instead of the multi-channel ideal. Lack of the sufficient quality and quantity of informational input can result in problems in learning ranging from language and learning disabilities to mental retardation.

Feedback

The feedback loop is the basic mechanism for the control of systems. Of the two types of feedback, one is internal to the system and the other is external. These types of feedback can be either positive, maintaining the growth and survival of a system, or negative, supplying information that a system is off course or out of bounds. Internal feedback loops regulate the functioning of the physical body and operate so automatically we hardly notice; for example, in the control of respiration and body temperature.

Feedback circuits maintain psychological and social system functioning, too. In the first relationship of infant and mother, each provides feedback to the other. Mother's touch and smile reward Baby, and Baby's coo and gaze reward Mother. It may be Baby, in fact, who is the more influential of the two. This is particularly apparent with a baby whose differences dramatically affect the relationship, such as one who is blind or one of difficult temperament.

By his or her very presence, a baby influences the functioning of the entire family system. While families shape babies, babies also shape families. By means of positive feedback, families encourage certain behaviors in their children, and by negative feedback, discourage others. Expectations on the part of parents for certain behaviors—cooperation, sharing, toilet training—serve to keep baby on course to becoming a socialized being.

Vital Balance

A healthy system maintains a vital balance among its subsystems and with its environment. The biological, psychological, and social systems of a child exist in a state of dynamic interaction, so that when a disturbance occurs in any one of the systems, the balance of the whole is affected. Following an upset, regulatory circuits strive to return the system to its original state. A system's ability to recover its balance depends upon internal and external resources which can be rallied.

The natural response of a family when distress interferes with their child's ability to learn, is to attempt to right the disturbance.

One way to temporarily restore balance is to change family attitudes about the problem. For example, a mother may convince herself that her son, Jeremy, who is two and not talking, is not, in fact, delayed in development ("My brother, Henry, was slow in talking, and he turned out fine," or "Jeremy will talk when he's ready, and he's just not ready yet.") The family may take action in the hope of remedying the problem, such as putting Jeremy in a day care center for contact with other children of his age, or insisting that Grandmother stop talking "baby talk" to him.

In some cases, home remedies do work. A child may either be given some extra time to develop unhindered or extra input needed to stimulate a specific area of development. However, when a family's attempts to regain balance fail, it is usually then that they seek an evaluation.

The first step in any evaluation is to take a detailed history of a child's development. To keep fresh in our minds the process of normal development, let's look once again at Lyle, Jr., this time interweaving the biological, psychological, and social threads of his development, instead of teasing them apart.

LYLE'S DEVELOPMENT

Birth

Birth marks a major transition from growth within the womb to growth without. At birth, human babies are not finished products, and they have a great deal of developing left to accomplish.

The interaction begun with Mother in the womb now turns into face-to-face interaction with her and with other members of the nuclear family. For most babies, Mother is the primary caretaker and love object. Fathers play varying parts with baby, depending upon their social status, race, and family background.

Lyle spends time immediately following birth with both of his parents. This time together encourages their bonding into a family unit. At barely one month old, Lyle already has the reputation of being even-tempered because of his regularity in feeding, sleeping, and eliminating.

Three Months

Attachment is well underway. Lyle is alert, cuddly, and easy to console, and these characteristics encourage the bonding process. He appears fascinated by the mobiles suspended over his crib, and when placed on his stomach, he lifts his head for a better look. Lyle quickly spots new visual stimuli around him, and just the sight of Susan's nipple alerts him that it is feeding time. Already a social being, he protests when put down or left alone. His smile can be brought on by the sight of Mother's face or by a "gittcheegoo" from Dad.

Six Months

Cooing has given way to babbling. Lyle "talks" in turn with inflection and expression. He now sits in a high chair in the kitchen at meal time. He likes to feed himself crackers, and he seems to relish looking at objects turned upside down—a cup, a plate, his bowl of oatmeal. Once she tires of cleaning up the mess around his high chair, Susan buys feeding bowls with suction cups on the bottom. It is now easy to read Lyle's emotional state—he gurgles and laughs when contented, screams and turns red when upset.

Nine Months

Lyle is now crawling and exploring his surroundings. He understands a few single words—"shoe," "no," "bye"—and a couple of two-word combinations which he processes as one word—"BabyLyle," "goodboy." He delights in hearing "baby talk" from his mother, father, and grandparents. The intonation and repetition of words like "choo-choo" and "tum-tum" convey to Lyle that talking is fun. His accomplished thumb-finger grasp makes it easy for him to pluck raisins from a box. Also, he is beginning to drink from a cup, rarely missing his mark. Attachment to Mother is complete, so that Lyle clouds up if Susan leaves the room unexpectedly.

Twelve Months

Lyle's understanding of words leads naturally to his trying out words of his own. He begins naming the people and possessions in his environment which are significant to him—"mama," "dada," "nana" for Grandma, "sock," "doll," and "binkie" for his favorite blanket. Up and walking, Lyle flies through the house. It seems to Susan that she has turned her back only for a minute to find that Lyle has managed to pull off his socks and shoes, dump over a basketful of clean laundry, or empty a drawer from his dresser.

Eighteen Months

Words are coming now in a rush. Lyle continues to relate to his surroundings in a primarily visual way, preferring to explore with his eyes and hands. His favorite toys are blocks, a shape ball, and a pull-toy duck on wheels. As Lyle begins his psychological separation from his mother, he is becoming more aware of himself as a person, claiming his possessions and defining his territory with "Mine!" He requires less attention from his parents at meal time. Lyle now uses a spoon, spilling very little.

Two Years

Two-word combinations abound. There are lots of activities in Lyle's life and, therefore, lots to talk about. Lyle likes to be on the move, especially outdoors. When his cousins come over to play, he plays beside them, sometimes glancing over to watch them. No areas of the house are off limits now, because Lyle can easily manage handles and doorknobs. His favorite toys are puzzles and a tool bench. For the first time, he is choosing going out with Dad over staying home with Mother.

Three Years

Lyle is introduced to table activities at preschool. He likes working with his hands, so Susan supplies him with a little table, crayons, finger paints, and scissors at home. Lyle is becoming more and more independent. He washes his hands by himself and blows his nose when reminded, although he still needs some help with dressing. His preschool experiences have taught him the meaning of the words "share" and "take turns." Since he is an only child, these words are new to his vocabulary.

Four Years

Lyle is spending more time in fantasy and role play. He plays house and dress-up with his cousin, Madeleine, and likes to act out scenes from movies he's seen. He has mastered buttoning and, for the most part, dresses himself. He still occasionally gets his shirt on backward with the tag in the front. Lyle has a strong sense of who he is. He can tell his street address, home town, and telephone number, and is beginning to define his likes and dislikes.

Five Years

Kindergarten is a challenge that Lyle meets with ease. He is able to stay in his seat for extended periods, and his attention span is good. He adapts easily to seat work and enjoys the workbooks and art projects. He is also adept at neighborhood activities such as catch, somersaults, and roller skating. When going to a neighbor's to play, Lyle crosses the street by himself.

School Years

For Lyle, the transition from preschool to school is easily made. Lyle demonstrates his ability to take on roles in a variety of social settings—at birthday parties for friends, at family get-togethers, and on his softball team. Math comes automatically to Lyle, but he requires a bit of extra help from Susan to grasp what is expected in reading and spelling. Once he does, however, he excels in these areas, too.

Lyle's development has unfolded evenly and effortlessly. Unlike Lyle, children who experience distress in one of their developing systems will be slowed or halted in the learning process. Red flags signalling that a disturbance is occurring include failure to meet

milestones and case history events usually related to a disturbance. When a family lacks the resources to cope with their child's
disturbance, they usually reach out to community resources and
seek an evaluation.

EVALUATION

The first question to be answered by evaluation is **which system
of the child is the primary system disturbed?** Remember, the **primary**
system disturbed refers to the primary one in **importance.** This is
the system most disturbed and the one which will demand the
most immediate intervention as well as the most resources of time,
energy, and money. **Primary** also refers to the first in **time,** meaning
that the disturbance originated within that system. In most cases,
the two are one and the same, i.e., the system most disturbed is
also the system from which the disturbance originated.

It may surprise you now to find that of the questions dealt with
in evaluation, this is probably the least important one. This is
because the answer is so dependent upon the point of view of the
examiner. In the case of Benjamin, the blind baby from Chapter
11, the developmental psychologist who tested him perceived the
primary system disturbance to be the **social system.** Because of his
background in working with families of blind children, he was
most attuned to family discord. The Farmers' family doctor might
have focused upon the **biological system** disturbance because of the
baby's blindness. A child psychiatrist might have seen a **psychological
system** disturbance because of the breakdown in the mother-child
relationship.

While it is not critical for a child's wellbeing that professionals
agree about the primary system disturbed, it is critical for them to
have a systems perspective. Only then is it possible for a child to
receive treatment at all levels of system which require it.

The system most disturbed does not **always** correspond with the
one first disturbed. For example, the system most disturbed in
autistic children is considered by most professionals to be the
psychological system. However, there has been disagreement about
whether the disturbance originates within the biological system,

caused perhaps by a birth injury, or the psychological system, brought on by a rejecting mother.

Even when the first system disturbed can be pinpointed, this does not mean the handicapping condition can be traced to a specific point of distress within the developing system. For example, cerebral palsy comes about only by distress to the biological system. However, it can be produced at any of these developmental points: at conception, in the womb, or at birth.

Many handicapping conditions which correspond with special education labels can result from a disturbance which begins in the biological, psychological, or social systems, as Table 12-I shows. For example, a disturbance originating in any of the systems can lead to retardation, learning disabilities, or emotional disturbance.

Table 12-I
HANDICAPPING CONDITIONS WHICH RESULT FROM A DISTURBANCE
ORIGINATING IN THE BIOLOGICAL, PSYCHOLOGICAL, OR SOCIAL SYSTEM

Handicapping Condition	Biological System	Psychological System	Social System
Mental Retardation	●	●	●
Hearing Impairment	●	○	○
Visual Impairment	●	○	○
Speech/Language Disorder	●	●	●
Learning Disability	●	●	●
Physical Handicap	●	○	○
Emotional Disturbance	●	●	●

The second step in evaluation is to estimate the relative influence of template and environment upon learning. The professionals who do psychological and educational testing are developmental psychologists, child psychologists, speech-language pathologists, and psychometrists.

There is a dynamic balance between genetic information programmed into a child's template and the information available in a child's physical and social environment. Both affect ability to learn. While the template sets a range of intellectual possibilities for a child, environmental input can nudge the child to upper

Figure 12-1. A goal of evaluation is to determine the relative influence of template and environment upon a child's ability to learn.

limits of potential. From crib to classroom, it is important to determine whether or not the child has received sufficient types and amounts of information, and it is important to know a child's range of intelligence for proper classroom placement.

The third step in an evaluation is to **describe the child's individual learning style.** Lyle and his cousins, Madeleine and Carl, illustrate the three basic types of learners. Each prefers a different type of input and a different means of expression. Lyle, the **looker,** prefers visual information and uses his hands for expression. In contrast, Madeline, the **listener,** favors auditory information and communicates best with words. Carl, the **mover,** chooses tactile information and expresses himself with large motor movements and social interaction.

The task of the evaluator is to describe the child's favored way of learning and make suggestions for how the child can best be taught. This information helps the teacher design an individualized teaching plan.

Figure 12-2. Another goal of evaluation is to determine a child's preferred learning style—looker, listener, or mover.

Last, the evaluator **lists the steps to be taken to encourage wellbeing at all levels of system.** The child's master plan for treatment will involve referrals to one or a number of specialists who can provide therapeutic services to the child and family.

Both **process**-and **content**-oriented therapy may be required—process therapy to ready the child to learn and content therapy to teach specific skills.

Examples of types of referrals which may be necessary for **biological system** distress are: referral to a pediatric neurologist for medication for seizures, to a developmental optometrist for eye exercises, and to an audiologist for the fitting of a hearing aid. Types of **psychological system** interventions include individual psychotherapy for mother and child, and outlets to help build a child's self-confidence, such as Scouts or music lessons. Typically, **social system** treatments increase a family's links to other social systems and could include language therapy, a softball team, and Parents Without Partners.

A child's master plan is never complete. It changes as the needs of child and family change and as community resources become available. The primary goal of all types of treatment is to help children grow, pushing the outside limits of their potential.

* * * * * *

BIBLIOGRAPHY

Adams, R. D., and Lyon, G. *Neurology of Hereditary Metabolic Diseases of Children.* Washington, D.C.: Hemisphere, 1982.

Adler, S. *Poverty Children and Their Language: Implications for Teaching and Treating.* New York: Grune and Stratton, 1979.

Allport, G. W. *Pattern and Growth in Personality.* New York: Holt, Rinehart, Winston, 1961.

American Psychiatric Association. *Diagnostic and Statistical Manual of Mental Disorders (DSM—III).* 3rd ed. Washington, D.C.: American Psychiatric Association, 1980.

Ames, L. B. *Is Your Child in the Wrong Grade?* Lumberville, Pennsylvania: Modern Learning Press, 1978.

Anastasiow, N. J., Hanes, M. L., and Hanes, M. L. *Language and Reading Strategies for Poverty Children.* Baltimore: University Park Press, 1982.

Anthony, E. J. "How Children Cope with a Psychotic Parent." In E. N. Rexford, L. W. Sander, and T. Shapiro (Eds.), *Infant Psychiatry: A New Synthesis.* New Haven: Yale University Press, 1976.

Barsch, R. H. *Enriching Perception and Cognition: Techniques for Teachers.* Vol. 2. Seattle: Special Child Publications, 1968.

Beavers, W. R. *Family Variables Related to the Development of a Self.* Report No. 68. Dallas: Timberlawn Foundation, 1972.

Bertalanffy, L. von. "General Systems Theory." *General Systems Yearbook* 1(1956):1–9.

Bertalanffy, L. von. "General Systems Theory—A Critical Overview." *General Systems Yearbook* 7(1962):1–20.

Bertalanffy, L. von. *General Systems Theory.* New York: Braziller, 1968.

Bertalanffy, L. von. P. A. LaViolette (Ed.) *A Systems View of Man.* Boulder: Westview Press, 1981.

Birdwhistell, R. L. *Kinesics and Context.* Philadelphia: University of Pennsylvania Press, 1970.

Blakeslee, T. R. *The Right Brain: A New Understanding of the Unconscious Mind and Its Creative Powers.* Garden City: Anchor, 1980.

Bohm, D. *Wholeness and the Implicate Order.* London: Routledge and Kegan Paul, 1980.

Bouchard, T. J., Jr. "Genetic Factors in Intelligence." In A. R. Kaplan (Ed.), *Human Behavior Genetics.* Springfield: Charles C Thomas, 1976.

Boulding, K. E. "General Systems Theory—The Skeleton of a Science." *General*

Systems Yearbook 1(1956):3–10.

Bower, E. M. *Early Identification of Emotionally Handicapped Children in School.* 2nd ed. Springfield: Charles C Thomas, 1969.

Bowlby, J. *Attachment and Loss: Separation.* New York: Basic Books, 1973.

Brazelton, T. B. *Neonatal Behavioral Assessment Scale.* Philadelphia: J. B. Lippincott, 1973.

Brody, J. *Jane Brody's Nutrition Book: A Lifetime Guide to Good Eating for Better Health and Weight Control.* New York: W. W. Norton, 1981.

Brofenbrenner, U. "Who Cares for America's Children." In V. C. Vaughn and T. B. Brazelton (Eds.), *The Family — Can It Be Saved?* Chicago: Year Book Medical Publications, 1976.

Brofenbrenner, U. *The Ecology of Human Development: Experiments by Nature and Design.* Cambridge: Harvard University Press, 1979.

Brostrøm, K. "Human Milk and Infant Formulas: Nutritional and Immunological Characteristics." In R. M. Suskind (Ed.), *Textbook of Pediatric Nutrition.* New York: Raven, 1981.

Bzoch, K. R. (Ed.) *Communicative Disorders Related to Cleft Lip and Palate.* Boston: Little, Brown, 1979.

Cantor, S. *The Schizophrenic Child.* Montreal: Eden Press, 1982.

Carlile, G. B. "A Multilevel Systems Approach to the Analysis of the Temporal Patterns in the Diadic Communication of Language Delayed Normal Four Year Olds." Unpublished doctoral dissertation, University of Oklahoma, 1980.

Cartwright, D., and Zander, A. *Group Dynamics: Research and Theory.* New York: Harper and Row, 1968.

Cruickshank, W. M. *Cerebral Palsy: A Developmental Disability.* Syracuse: Syracuse University Press, 1976.

Cruz, F. F. de la, and Gerald, P. S. *Trisomy 21 (Down Syndrome): Research Perspectives.* Baltimore: University Park Press, 1981.

Darley, F. L. *Evaluation of Appraisal Techniques in Speech and Language Pathology.* Reading: Addison-Wesley, 1979.

Davidson, M. *Uncommon Sense: The Life and Thought of Ludwig von Bertalanffy (1901-1972) Father of General Systems Theory.* Los Angeles: J. P. Tarcher, 1983.

Delacato, C. H. *The Diagnosis and Treatment of Speech and Reading Problems.* Springfield: Charles C Thomas, 1963.

Deutsch, M. "The Disadvantaged Child and the Learning Process." In M. Deutsch (Ed.), *The Disadvantaged Child.* New York: Basic Books, 1967.

DiLeo, J. H. *Children's Drawings as Diagnostic Aids.* New York: Brunner/Mazel, 1973.

Dillard, J. L. *Black English.* New York: Random House, 1972.

Dossey, L. *Space, Time, and Medicine.* Boulder: Shambhala, 1982.

Dunn, L. M., and Dunn, L. M. *Manual for the Peabody Picture Vocabulary Test.* Circle Pines, Minnesota: American Guidance Service, 1981.

Edwards, B. *Drawing on the Right Side of the Brain.* Los Angeles: J. P. Tarcher, 1979.

Elam, D. *Building Better Babies.* Millbrae, California: Cellestial Arts, 1980.

Elkind, D. *The Hurried Child: Growing Up Too Fast Too Soon.* Reading, Massachusetts: Addison-Wesley, 1981.

Escalona, S. K. *The Roots of Individuality.* Chicago: Aldine, 1968.

Farb, P. *Word Play: What Happens When People Talk.* New York: Knopf, 1974.

Fay, W. H., and Schuler, A. L. *Emerging Language in Autistic Children.* Baltimore: University Park Press, 1980.

Feingold, B. F., and Feingold, H. S. *The Feingold Cookbook for Hyperactive Children.* New York: Random House, 1979.

Fraiberg, S. "Blind Infants and Their Mothers: An Examination of the Sign System." In M. Lewis and L. A. Rosenblum (Eds.), *The Effect of the Infant on Its Caregiver.* Vol. 1. New York: John Wiley, 1974.

Fraiberg, S. *Every Child's Birthright: In Defense of Mothering.* New York: Basic Books, 1977.

Frankenburg, W. K., Dodds, J. B., and Fandal, A. W. *Manual for the Denver Developmental Screening Test.* Denver: University of Colorado Medical Center, 1970.

Garvey, C. *Play.* Cambridge: Harvard University Press, 1977.

Gazzaniga, M. S., and LeDoux, J. E. *The Integrated Mind.* New York: Plenum, 1978.

Gelles, R. J. "Child Abuse and Family Violence: Implications for Medical Professionals." In E. H. Newberger (Ed.), *Child Abuse.* Boston: Little, Brown, 1982.

Gerras, C. *The Complete Book of Vitamins.* Emmaus: Rodale Press, 1977.

Goffman, E. *Stigma: Notes on the Management of Spoiled Identity.* Englewood Cliffs: Prentice-Hall, 1963.

Gould, S. J. *The Mismeasure of Man.* New York: Norton, 1981.

Gray, W. "Ludwig von Bertalanffy and the Development of Modern Psychiatric Thought." In W. Gray and N. D. Rizzo (Eds.), *Unity Through Diversity.* Vol. I. New York: Gordon and Breach, 1973.

Gray, W., Duhl, F. J., and Rizzo, N. D. (Eds.). *General Systems Theory and Psychiatry.* 2nd ed. Seaside, California: Intersystems Publications, 1981.

Grunebaum, H., Weiss, J. L., Cohler, B. J., Hartman, C. R., and Gallant, D. H. *Mentally Ill Mothers and Their Children.* Chicago: University of Chicago Press, 1975.

Guze, S. B., Earls, F. J., and Barrett, J. E. (Eds.). *Childhood Psychopathology and Development.* New York: Raven Press, 1983.

Hetherington, E. M., Cox, M., and Cox, R. "The Development of Children in Mother-Headed Families." In D. Reiss and H. A. Hoffman, *The American Family: Dying or Developing.* New York: Plenum Press, 1979.

Hoopes, A., and Hoopes, T. *Eye Power.* New York: Alfred A. Knopf, 1979.

Ilg, F., Ames, L. B., Haines, J., and Gillespie, C. *School Readiness.* New York: Harper and Row, 1978.

Illingworth, R. S. "The Development of Communication in the First Year and the Factors which Affect It." In T. Murry and J. Murry (Eds.), *Infant Communication: Cry and Early Speech.* Houston: College-Hill Press, 1980.

Jackson, D. D. (Ed.). *Communication, Family, and Marriage.* Palo Alto: Science and Behavior Books, 1968.

Jackson, D. D. "The Individual and the Larger Contexts." In W. Gray, F. J. Duhl, and N. D. Rizzo (Eds.), *General Systems Theory and Psychiatry.* Seaside, California: Intersystems Publications, 1981.

Jantsch, E. "Unifying Principles of Evolution." In E. Jantsch (Ed.), *The Evolutionary Vision: Toward a Unifying Paradigm of Physical, Biological, and Sociocultural Evolution.* Boulder: Westview Press, 1981.

Jensen, M., Benson, R. C., and Bobak, I. M. *Maternity Care: The Nurse and the Family.* St. Louis: C. V. Mosby Co., 1977.

Jones, R. A. *Self-fulfilling Prophecies: Social, Psychological and Physiological Effects of Expectancies.* Hillsdale: Lawrence Erlbaum, 1977.

Kaplan, L. J. *Oneness and Separateness: From Infant to Individual.* New York: Simon and Schuster, 1978.

Kaye, K. *The Mental and Social Life of Babies: How Parents Create Persons.* Chicago: University of Chicago Press, 1982.

Klaus, M. H., and Kennell, J. H. *Maternal-Infant Bonding.* St. Louis: C. V. Mosby Co., 1976.

Klaus, M. H., and Kennell, J. H. *Parent-Infant Bonding.* 2nd ed. St. Louis: C. V. Mosby Co., 1982.

Koegel, R. L., Rincover, A., and Engel, A. L. *Educating and Understanding Autistic Children.* San Diego: College-Hill, 1982.

Korner, A. F. "Conceptual Issues in Infancy Research." In J. D. Osofsky (Ed.), *Handbook of Infant Development.* New York: John Wiley, 1979.

Krishef, C. H. *An Introduction to Mental Retardation.* Springfield, Ill.: Charles C Thomas, 1983.

Laosa, Luis M. "Nonbiased Assessment of Children's Abilities: Historical Antecedents and Current Issues." In T. Oakland (Ed.), *Psychological and Educational Assessment of Minority Children.* New York: Brunner/Mazel, 1977.

Leboyer, F. *Birth Without Violence.* New York: Alfred A. Knopf, 1976.

Levine, J. A. *Who Will Raise the Children?* Philadelphia: J. B. Lippincott Co., 1976.

Levine, J. A. "Real Kids Vs. 'The Average' Family." *Psychology Today* 12(1978):14–15.

Lewis, M., and Rosenblum, L. A. (Eds.). *The Effect of the Infant on Its Caregiver.* Vol. 1. New York: John Wiley, 1974.

Lewis, O. *Families.* New York: Basic Books, 1959.

Lowen, A. *Bioenergetics.* New York: Coward, McCann and Geoghegan, 1975.

Lynn, D. B. *The Father: His Role in Child Development.* Monterey, Calif.: Brooks/Cole, 1974.

McCall, R. B. "Prenatal Development." In R. E. Schell (Ed.), *Developmental Psychology Today.* 2nd ed. New York: Random House, 1975.

McFarland, J. C. "A Systems Approach to Human Communication." In D. E. Washburn and D. R. Smith (Eds.), *Coping With Increasing Complexity.* New York: Gordon and Breach, 1974.

MacFarlane, A. *The Psychology of Childbirth.* Cambridge: Harvard University Press, 1977.

McWilliams, M. *Nutrition for the Growing Years.* 2nd ed. New York: John Wiley, 1971.

Mahler, M. S., Pine, F., and Bergman, A. *The Psychological Birth of the Human Infant.* New York: Basic Books, 1975.

Martin, F. *Pediatric Audiology.* Englewood Cliffs, N. J.: Prentice-Hall, 1978.

Mauser, A. *Assessing the Learning Disabled: Selected Instruments.* Novato, Calif.: Academic Therapy Publications, 1977.

May, R. *Sex and Fantasy: Patterns of Male and Female Development.* Wideview, 1980.

Mecham, M. J. *Verbal Language Development Scale.* Circle Pines, Minn.: American Guidance Service, 1971.

Meerloo, J. A. M. *The Dance.* Philadelphia: Chilton, 1960.

Menninger, K. (with M. Mayman and P. Pruyser). *The Vital Balance.* New York: Viking Press, 1963.

Merton, R. K. "The Self-Fulfilling Prophecy." *Antioch Review* 8(1948):193–210.

Miller, J. G. "Toward a General Theory for the Behavioral Sciences." *American Psychologist* 10(1955):513–531.

Miller, J. G. *Living Systems.* New York: McGraw-Hill, 1978.

Miller, J. G. "Living Systems: Basic Concepts." In W. Gray, F. J. Duhl, Rizzo, N. D. (Eds.), *General Systems Theory and Psychiatry.* Seaside, Calif.: Intersystems, 1981.

Montagu, A. *Prenatal Influences.* Springfield, Ill.: Charles C Thomas, 1962.

Montagu, A. *Touching: The Human Significance of the Skin.* 2nd Ed. New York: Harper and Row, 1978.

Moore, K. L. *The Developing Human: Clinically Oriented Embryology.* 3rd Ed. Philadelphia: W. B. Saunders, 1982.

Oakland, T. (Ed.). *Psychological and Educational Assessment of Minority Children.* New York: Brunner/Mazel, 1977.

Ornstein, R. E. *The Psychology of Consciousness.* 2nd ed. New York: Harcourt, Brace, Jovanovich, 1977.

Osofsky, J. D. (Ed.). *Handbook of Infant Development.* New York: John Wiley, 1979.

Osofsky, J. D., and Connors, K. "Mother-Infant Interactions: An Integrative View of a Complex System." In J. D. Osofsky (Ed.), *Handbook of Infant Development.* New York: John Wiley, 1979.

Padus, E. *The Woman's Encyclopedia of Health and Natural Healing.* Emmaus: Rodale Press, 1981.

Parsons, T. "General Theory in Sociology." In R. K. Merton (Ed.), *Sociology Today: Problems and Prospects.* New York: Harper and Row, 1959.

Parsons, T., and Bales, R. F. *Family, Socialization and Interaction Process.* Glencoe, Ill.: The Free Press, 1955.

Patlee, H. H. "Symbol-Structure Complementarity in Biological Evolution." In E. Jantsch (Ed.), *Toward a Unifying Paradigm of Physical, Biological, and Sociocultural Evolution.* Boulder: Westview, 1981.

Pietsch, P. *Shufflebrain.* Boston: Houghton Mifflin, 1981.

Pines, M. "Superkids." *Psychology Today* 12(1979):52–63.

Pulaski, M. A. "The Rich Rewards of Make Believe." *Psychology Today* 7(1974):68–74.

Quay, H. C., and Werry, J. S. (Eds.). *Psychopathological Disorders of Childhood.* New York: John Wiley, 1972.

Rapaport, A. "Modern Systems Theory—An Outlook for Coping with Change." *General Systems Yearbook* 40(1970):15–25.

Restak, R. M. *The Brain: The Last Frontier.* Garden City, N.Y.: Doubleday, 1979.

Rexford, E. N., Sander, L. W., and Shapiro, T. (Eds.). *Infant Psychiatry: A New Synthesis.* New Haven: Yale University Press, 1976.

Rosenthal, R. "The Pygmalion Effect Lives." *Psychology Today* 7(1973):56–60.

Rosenthal, R., and Jacobson, L. "Teachers' Expectancies: Determinants of Pupils' IQ Gains." *Psychological Reports* 19(1966):115–118.

Rosenthal, R., and Jacobson, L. "Self-fulfilling Prophecies in the Classroom: Teacher expectations as Unintended Determinants of Pupils' Intellectual Competence." In M. Deutsch (Ed.), *Social Class, Race, and Psychological Development.* New York: Holt, Rinehart and Winston, 1967.

Rosenthal, R., and Jacobson, L. *Pygmalion in the Classroom: Teacher Expectation and Pupils' Intellectual Development.* New York: Holt, Rinehart and Winston, 1968a.

Rosenthal, R., and Jacobson, L. "Teacher Expectations for the Disadvantaged." *Scientific American* 218(1968b):19–23.

Royce, J. R. "Personality as an Adaptive System." In W. Gray, J. Fidler, and J. Battista (Eds.), *General Systems Theory and the Psychological Sciences* Vol. 2. Seaside, Calif.: Intersystems, 1982.

Rueveni, U., Speck, R. V., and Speck, J. L. *Therapeutic Intervention: Healing Strategies for Human Systems.* New York: Human Sciences Press, 1982.

Rugh, R., and Shettles, L. *From Conception to Birth: The Drama of Life's Beginnings.* New York: Harper and Row, 1971.

Samples, B. *The Metaphoric Mind: A Celebration of Creative Consciousness.* Reading: Addison-Wesley, 1976.

Sarbin, T. R. "The Culture of Poverty, Social Identity, and Cognitive Outcomes." In V. L. Allen (Ed.), *Psychological Factors in Poverty.* Chicago: Markham, 1970.

Satir, V. *Peoplemaking.* Palo Alto, Calif.: Science and Behavior Books, 1972.

Scarr-Salapatek, S., and Salapatek, P. (Eds.). *Socialization.* Columbus, Ohio: Charles Merrill, 1973.

Schwartz, L. *The World of the Unborn: Nurturing Your Child Before Birth.* New York: Marek, 1980.

Scipien, G. M., Barnard, M. U., Chard, M. A., Howe, J., and Phillips, P. J. *Comprehensive Pediatric Nursing.* 2nd ed. New York: McGraw-Hill, 1979.

Sherif, M., and Sherif, C. W. "Properties of Groups." *An Outline of Social Psychology.* New York: Harper and Row, 1956.

Smith, D. W. "Mechanical Forces and Patterns of Deformation." In T. G. Connelly, L. L. Brinkley, and B. M. Carlson (Eds.), *Morphogenesis and Pattern Formation.* New York: Raven, 1981.

Spitz, R. A. *The First Year of Life.* New York: International Universities Press, 1965.

Springer, N. S. *Nutrition Casebook on Developmental Disabilities.* Syracuse, N.Y.: Syracuse University Press, 1982.

Springer, S. P., and Deutsch, G. *Left Brain, Right Brain.* San Francisco: Freeman, 1981.

Sroufe, L. A. "Socioemotional Development." In J. D. Osofsky (Ed.), *Handbook of Infant Development.* New York: John Wiley, 1979.

Stern, D. *The First Relationship: Mother and Infant.* Cambridge: Harvard University Press, 1977.

Teyler, T. J. "The Brain Sciences: An Introduction." In J. S. Chall, and A. F. Mirsky (Eds.), *Education and the Brain.* Chicago: University of Chicago Press, 1978.

Thomas, A. "Behavioral Individuality in Childhood." In A. R. Kaplan (Ed.), *Human Behavior Genetics.* Springfield, Ill.: Charles C Thomas, 1976.

Verny, T. *The Secret Life of the Unborn Child.* New York: Summit Books, 1981.

Virshup, E. *Right Brain People in a Left Brain World.* Los Angeles: Guild of Tutors Press, 1978.

Walsh, R. *Towards an Ecology of Brain.* New York: SP Medical and Scientific Books, 1981.

Warkany, J., Lemire, R. J., and Cohen, M. M., Jr. *Mental Retardation and Congenital Malformation of the Central Nervous System.* Chicago: Year Book Medical Publishers, 1981.

Watzlawick, P., Beavin, J. H., and Jackson, D. D. *Pragmatics of Human Communication.* New York: W. W. Norton, 1967.

Wechsler, D. *Manual for the Wechsler Preschool and Primary Scale of Intelligence.* New York: The Psychological Corporation, 1967.

Wechsler, D. *Manual for the Wechsler Intelligence Scale for Children* (Revised). New York: The Psychological Corporation, 1974.

White, B. L. *The First Three Years of Life.* Englewood Cliffs, N.J.: Prentice-Hall, 1975.

GLOSSARY OF SYSTEMS TERMS

B

BIOLOGICAL SYSTEM: The physical body bounded by the skin.

C

CYBERNETICS: The science of control mechanisms.

E

ENVIRONMENT: That which surrounds and supports a system.
EXTERNAL FEEDBACK: A feedback loop which exits through the output boundary, passes through the environment, and re-enters at the input boundary.

F

FEEDBACK: Communication network which permits systems to manage internal functions and make external adjustments to the environment.

H

HARD SCIENCES: Exact sciences, e.g., physics, chemistry, mathematics.
HEREDITARY INPUTS: Information programmed into the template which establishes certain limits and/or patterns of learning.
HOMEOSTASIS: A living system's process of self-regulation and return to balance following a disturbance.

I

INFORMATION: Refers both to the data which enters a living system and to the communication network within the system for handling the data.
INPUT: That which comes into a system, matter-energy or information.
INTERNAL FEEDBACK: A feedback loop which is wholly internal to a system, i.e., a closed loop which does not cross the system boundary.

L

LIVING SYSTEMS: A special subset of all possible systems; specifically, plants, animals, groups, organizations, societies, and supranational systems.

N

NEGATIVE FEEDBACK: Supplies information to a system that it is off course or out of bounds.

O

OPEN SYSTEMS: Those systems which readily permit inputs from the environment to cross their boundaries; synonymous with living systems.

OUTPUT: That which leaves a system and can be observed.

P

POSITIVE FEEDBACK: Maintains growth and survival of the system.

PSYCHOLOGICAL SELF: Personality; that part of an individual which is separate from the roles he or she plays.

PSYCHOLOGICAL SYSTEM: Bounded first by mother and baby, out of this relationship a child's personality emerges; the personality then becomes the boundary of the psychological system.

R

REGULATORY MECHANISMS: Those mechanisms designed to counteract disturbances of a system which occur from within and/or without.

ROLE: The expected behavior of an individual in a group setting; the smallest unit of a social system.

S

SOCIAL SYSTEM: Refers to the social groups which a child takes part in, beginning with the nuclear and extended families and reaching out to include neighborhood, school, and community.

SOFT SCIENCES: Those which deal with the study of man, e.g., psychology, sociology, social psychology, anthropology.

SUBSYSTEM: The next lower level of a living system which carries out a particular function for the system.

SUPRASYSTEM: The next higher level of a system of which a living system is a part.

SYSTEM: A set of units with relationships among them.

SYSTEM DISTURBANCE: Inputs which, because of lack or excess, upset the natural balance of a system.

SYSTEMS PERSPECTIVE: When pertaining to handicapped children, refers to the importance of evaluating all systems of a child—biological, psychological, and social—instead of isolating one system for study.

T

TEMPLATE: The original blueprint of the structure of a system from the moment of conception; in living systems, it contains genetic information.

THROUGHPUT: Information as it is processed within a system.

V

VITAL BALANCE: The dynamic interaction between a living system and its environment.

GLOSSARY OF PROFESSIONALS

ALLERGIST: Medical doctor who diagnoses and treats allergic diseases in children.

ART THERAPIST: Holds master's degree in art therapy; employs art as a therapeutic medium for work with children; may use art as an adjunct to psychotherapy.

AUDIOLOGIST: Holds master's degree in audiology; tests children's hearing, fits and repairs hearing aids; may provide oral rehabilitation and evaluate learning disabilities related to auditory processing disorders.

CHILD PSYCHIATRIST: Medical doctor specializing in the diagnosis and treatment of mental and emotional disorders in children. Uses play therapy, medication, and parent counseling as therapeutic techniques.

CHILD PSYCHOLOGIST: Holds doctorate in psychology; specializes in the diagnosis and treatment of mental and emotional disorders in children; administers and interprets psychological testing; sees children, parents, and families for psychotherapy.

CLINICAL PSYCHOLOGIST: Holds doctorate in psychology; works in a clinical setting such as an office, hospital, or mental health clinic. Depending upon work requirements, may play role of child or developmental psychologist or may work exclusively with adult patients who have emotional disorders.

DANCE THERAPIST: Holds master's degree in dance therapy; employs dance as a therapeutic medium in work with emotionally disturbed, mentally retarded, learning disabled, and physically disabled children. Plans programs to foster an awareness in children of their feelings and nonverbal behaviors.

DEVELOPMENTAL OPTOMETRIST: Doctor of optometry; examines vision in children, prescribes corrective lenses and/or eye exercises.

DEVELOPMENTAL PSYCHOLOGIST: Holds doctorate in psychology; administers and interprets psychological testing in clinical setting; specialist in normal child development and ways children learn.

GENETICIST: Medical doctor specializing in the detection and prevention of genetic defects in families.

LEARNING DISABILITY TEACHER: Holds bachelor's or master's degree in learning disabilities; works in a school setting and plans individualized instructional programs for children with learning disabilities; may teach in a self-contained classroom or a lab setting.

MOBILITY INSTRUCTOR: Holds bachelor's or master's degree in rehabilitation for the blind; evaluates the functional vision of the visually impaired; teaches orientation skills and cane travel.

MUSIC THERAPIST: Holds bachelor's or master's degree in music therapy; employs music as a therapeutic medium for work with children; may use music as an adjunct to psychotherapy.

NEONATOLOGIST: Medical doctor specializing in the diagnosis and treatment of medical problems of the newborn from birth to two months of age; often cares for premature infants.

NUTRITIONIST: Holds master's degree in nutrition; develops nutritional programs for children who require special diets, such as those who have food allergies or diabetes or who are overweight.

OCCUPATIONAL THERAPIST: Holds bachelor's or master's degree in occupational therapy. Usually works in a hospital setting with children who have physical and mental disabilities; teaches self-help, leisure, and social skills to children to promote independence in everyday living.

OPTHALMOLOGIST: Medical doctor specializing in the diagnosis and treatment of diseases of the eye.

OTOLARYNGOLOGIST: Medical doctor who treats diseases of the ear, nose, and throat in children.

PEDIATRICIAN: Medical doctor specializing in the diagnosis and treatment of childhood diseases and injuries.

PEDIATRIC NEUROLOGIST: Medical doctor specializing in the diagnosis and treatment of disorders of the nervous system in children.

PEDODONTIST: Dentist specializing in the dental care of children.

PHYSICAL THERAPIST: Holds bachelor's or master's degree in physical therapy; usually works in a hospital setting; helps children to improve or regain physical functioning through the use of massage and therapeutic exercises.

PLASTIC SURGEON: A surgeon who repairs physical defects, such as cleft lip and palate.

PSYCHOMETRIST: Holds master's degree in psychology; administers and interprets psychological testing in a school or clinical setting under the supervision of a doctorate-level psychologist.

SCHOOL PSYCHOLOGIST: Holds master's degree or doctorate in school psychology; administers and interprets psychological testing in a school setting; sees children individually for counseling and consults with classroom teachers.

SOCIAL WORKER: Holds master's degree in social work; often acts as intake worker in a clinic, interviewing a family first to clarify the nature of a child's problem in order to make appropriate referrals for testing. Also, may see one or more family members individually or as a group for therapy.

SPECIAL EDUCATION TEACHER: Holds bachelor's or master's degree in special education; usually works in a self-contained public school classroom teaching children who are in the educable or trainable range of retardation; term may also be used to refer to any teacher who provides specialized educational services.

SPEECH-LANGUAGE PATHOLOGIST: Holds master's degree in communication disorders; evaluates and provides therapy for children who have disorders of language, speech, voice, and articulation; diagnoses and remediates auditory disabilities in children; may work in schools, clinics, hospitals, or rehabilitation centers.

TEACHER OF THE BLIND: Holds bachelor's or master's degree in teaching the visually impaired; works in a public school setting, usually as a resource room teacher with children who are partially sighted or legally blind; uses braille, tapes, large print, and mobility techniques in classroom work.

TEACHER OF THE DEAF: Holds bachelor's or master's degree in deaf education; usually works in the public schools in a self-contained class or resource room; teaches communication skills (oral communication and signing) and academic subjects to the deaf and hearing-impaired.

TEACHER OF THE EMOTIONALLY DISTURBED: Holds bachelor's or master's degree in teaching the emotionally disturbed; works in a classroom setting with children who have been diagnosed as emotionally disturbed; teaches academic subjects, appropriate behaviors, and social skills.

INDEX

217